Great themes in Puritan preaching

A *tour de force* on Puritan preaching designed to do at least two things: to teach us of the centrality of preaching in Puritan piety, and to convince us of its value in our own world. This fine book proves for Christians what we should already know, but often fail to adequately grasp: preaching matters! A marvelous accomplishment!

Derek W. H. Thomas
John E. Richards Professor of Theology, Reformed Theological Seminary, Minister of Teaching, First Presbyterian Church, Jackson, Mississippi, Editorial Director, Alliance of Confessing Evangelicals

---

The Puritan era produced some of the finest, most enduring, most powerful preaching in the history of the church. There's a reason the best preachers in every subsequent era have usually looked back to the Puritans as their models: Puritan preaching was wonderfully clear, painstakingly precise, doctrinally meticulous—but above all, thoroughly biblical. Puritan messages flowed from the biblical text and therefore their themes invariably echoed the great themes of Scripture. Dr. Di Gangi has done a superb job of outlining and summarizing the dominant themes in Puritan preaching. You will learn much from this volume.

John MacArthur
Pastor of Grace Community Church, Sun Valley, California, President of Grace to You Ministries, The Master's College and The Master's Seminary

---

The writings of the English Puritans are a gold mine of both sound theology and instructions for practical Christian living. Unfortunately their preaching and writing style makes reading them difficult for twenty-first-century Christians. Dr. Mariano Di Gangi has done us a great service by giving us an abstract of their most significant teachings. Every Christian, but especially those of us in full-time ministry, will benefit greatly from this book.

Jerry Bridges
Author of over a dozen books including The Pursuit of Holiness, The Gospel for Real Life *and* The Joy of Fearing God

---

This primer on Puritan teaching ably expounds a variety of topics by some of the best Puritans, including John Owen on the infallibility of Scripture and justification, James Durham on the Ten Commandments, Thomas Watson on the offices of Christ, William Gouge on pastoral ministry and spiritual conflict, Arthur Hildersham on confession of sin, David Clarkson on the new birth, Richard Sibbes on repentance, Henry Smith on the Lord's Supper and family life, Thomas Horton on assurance, and David Dickson on the final judgement. Dr. Di Gangi writes simply, accurately, and winsomely—here is savory provision for both the beginner and the scholar of Puritan studies. And every believer will find great assistance in these pages for Christian faith and living.

Joel R. Beeke
Professor of Systematic Theology and Homiletics at Puritan Reformed Theological Seminary, Pastor of the Heritage Netherlands Reformed Congregation, Grand Rapids, Michigan, and Editor of The Banner of Sovereign Grace Truth

Other titles by the author

A Golden Treasury of Puritan Devotion
I Believe in Mission
King of Glory
Life & Immortality
Peter Martyr Vermigli: Renaissance Man, Reformation Master
The Spirit of Christ
Twelve Prophetic Voices
Understanding Handel's Messiah
Word For All Seasons

GREAT THEMES IN PURITAN PREACHING

Compiled and edited by Mariano Di Gangi

press

Joshua Press Inc.
Ontario, Canada
www.joshuapress.com

© 2007 by Joshua Press Inc.
All rights reserved. This book may not be reproduced, in whole or in part, without written permission from the publishers. Published 2007

Distributed by
Sola Scriptura Ministries International
www.sola-scriptura.ca

Editorial director: Michael A.G. Haykin
© Cover and book design by Janice Van Eck

COVER IMAGE The beloved Puritan divine, Dr. John Owen. Attributed to John Greenhill, oil on canvas, circa 1668 (NPG 115). © National Portrait Gallery, London.
LETTERFORMS This book is set in *17C Print OT* and *Janson Text*. *17C Print OT* is a font taken from a book published in 1686 (during the Puritan period). It incorporates not only the imperfections but also the art of seventeenth century printing.

Library and Archives Canada Cataloguing in Publication

    Great themes in Puritan preaching / compiled and edited by Mariano Di Gangi, 1923– , Sequel to A golden treasury of Puritan devotion.

ISBN 1-894400-24-0   ISBN-13 978-1-894400-24-4

    1. Puritans—Sermons—History and criticism. I. Di Gangi, Mariano

BX9323.G74 2007   251'.00882859   C2007-903771-2

PRINTED IN THE U.S.A.

In memory of my parents

Joseph & Rose Di Gangi

*who faithfully practiced
what the Puritans they never read
so eloquently preached*

Contents

	Foreword	11
	Preface	13
	Introduction	15
1	The infallible Word	19
2	No upstart sect	25
3	The Messiah revealed	33
4	Pastoral ministry	39
5	Guilt and grace	49
6	The second birth	55
7	Radical repentance	61
8	Justified and sanctified	67
9	Spiritual conflict	77
10	Bread and wine	87
11	Renewal and reform	93
12	Family values	99
13	Most blessed assurance	107
14	Advent to judgement	121
	Endnotes	129

Foreword

❦ ❦ ❦ ❦ ❦ ❦ ❦ ❦ ❦

The Puritans, as this fine work by Dr. Di Gangi clearly demonstrates, were preachers. Recent students of their thought have shown that they were also both advocates of national righteousness and guardians of the souls entrusted to them. But, first and foremost, they were preachers.

They were preachers because they rightly knew that through the Holy Scriptures God had brought the church into existence in the first century, kindling faith in the hearts of men and women (i.e. James 1:18; 1 Peter 1:22-25), and that it was through this selfsame Word that God had brought about the Reformation, which the earliest Puritans, of the 1560s and 1570s, could remember firsthand. And it was by the Word that God enabled men and women to live lives that glorified him, a key theme of Puritan thought.

The Reformation had involved a major shift of emphasis in the cultivation of Christian spirituality. Mediæval Roman Catholicism had majored on symbols and images as the means for cultivating spirituality. The Reformation, coming as it did hard on the heels of the invention of the printing press, turned back to the biblical emphasis on "words" as the primary vehicle of cultivating spirituality, both spoken words and written words, and, in particular, the words of the Bible. As faithful children of the Reformation, the Puritans simply continued this Reformation Word-centredness. It involved them in conflict, but they contended for their convictions and stood fast. Thus, when men like William Laud, the Archbishop of Canterbury, began to emphasize that the Lord's Supper was due greater reverence than the Word,[1] the Puritans knew that they had to stand against him and assert the priority of the Word and that in preaching.[2]

Like Puritanism, Evangelicalism has been strong when it has likewise sought to cultivate a faith that is first and foremost centred in the Scriptures. As John Cheeseman, the Anglican minister of Holy Trinity Church, Eastbourne, England, has recently noted, decadent periods of church history have "always" coincided with times when "the preaching of God's Word has been in decline."[3] Of course, we face challenges today in this regard. There are those who assert that words are no longer adequate. We need images and drama, they say. But, as the Puritans rightly knew, there can be no real substitute for the preaching of the Bible as the God-appointed means for the salvation of men and women and their ongoing edification.[4] Those congregations that surrender this God-given means of grace for other forms of communication more appealing to modern sensibilities are in danger of coming under the judgement of God and experiencing what Amos calls "a famine of the Word of God" (Amos 8:11-13).

The value of this book lies precisely in the way that Dr. Di Gangi brings out this all-important biblicism of the Puritans as well as detailing the variety of themes that appear in their sermonic literature. May it prove to be a word in season and convince its readers that preaching is as vital for our day, as it was for the Puritan era. ❦

Michael A.G. Haykin
June 8, 2007

Preface

This volume is a sequel to *A Golden Treasury of Puritan Devotion* (P & R Publishing, 1999) complied and edited by Mariano Di Gangi. Comparatively few words and phrases have been updated, and occasional connectives used to maintain continuity.

Appreciation is expressed to Jocelyne Dever, who turned the manuscript into a typescript in preparation for publication. Thanks is also due to the library of Tyndale College and Seminary, Toronto, for access to the Baldwin Collection of Puritan writings.

Introduction

Puritans have been caricatured by their critics as advocates of "the narrowest and most inquisitive clerical intolerance, a gloomy Calvinism in doctrine, Sabbatarianism in practice, and a degrading mental slavery to the mere letter of the Bible."[1] "Where once one might be accustomed to see an altar, leading his thoughts straightway to Jesus and to 'the Lamb in the midst of the elders as it had been slain,' he sees a cushioned pulpit... The noble liturgies of the early church have given way to the extempore effusions of an individual. The place of worship seems to have become a preaching house... Catholicity appears to have yielded to a bald French Calvinism, capable of imagining nothing but a sermon."[2] The Puritans were suspected of having "one eager all-absorbing passion—to Calvinize the Church of England and assimilate its polity and ritual—in all respects—to those of Scotland and Geneva."[3]

Undoubtedly, there may have been Dissenters whose extremist excesses produced intolerance rather than renewal in the turbulent decades that followed the Reformation. The fact remains, however, that "Puritanism aimed at a radical purification and reconstruction of church and state on the sole basis of the Word of God, without regard to the traditions of men... Radical in its antagonism to the medieval church, it was a revolution and it ran into the excesses of a revolution."[4]

The Puritans were people of austere morals, reformed in

doctrine, and nonconformists in practice when confronted with the imposition of ceremonies and customs not commanded in the Scriptures. Puritan preachers did not major in minors. They would not trivialize the tremendous truths that had the power to change lives. Building on the Nicene Creed, the Apostles' Creed, and the Christology of Chalcedon, they strongly opposed Pelagianism, Arminianism, and the Socinianism that eventually spawned Unitarianism. They also differed with the Antinomians who depreciated the authority of God's moral law. Nor would they compromise with the Semi-Pelagians who diluted the gospel of sovereign grace with doses of human merit.

Puritan theology, expressed in the *Westminster Confession of Faith* (1643-1648) and the *Savoy Declaration* (1658), was also in harmony with the *Scots' Confession* (1560), the *Belgic Confession* (1561) and the *Heidelberg Catechism* (1563) of the Reformation era. The Puritan movement was distinguished by a serious study of the Scriptures and the practical application of biblical doctrines. Accurate exegesis prepared the way for lively exposition and relevant conclusions. Puritan preachers "emphasized the importance of words in the text of Scripture... This wise and insightful use of words gave Puritan preaching an exactness and attractiveness that many other English pulpiteers lacked."[5]

The Puritans were noted not only for viewing the text in its context, and so avoiding a pretext, but also for comparing and contrasting biblical passages in such a way that Scripture was used to interpret Scripture. They knew how to distinguish between history and allegory and looked for Christ in texts that were typological. Above all, they believed that God's eternal Word was timely and trustworthy. It spoke to the ethical, social, and doctrinal issues faced by God's people in every generation. When the inspired Scripture is illumined by the Holy Spirit, it has an undoubted perspicuity.

It has been noted that "two emphases followed by the Puritans explain at least a part of their effectiveness... First, they educated the mind... They recognized that heat in the pulpit without light from the Scripture would not change people. Second, they appealed to an individual's relationship to God at each present moment. As they explained the Scriptures, they expected the Holy Spirit to honour their work by leading the hearers to judge themselves, and by producing response to the preaching."[6]

Puritanism developed as part of the Protestant Reformation in England. According to one writer, "Nonconformity was conceived during the days of King Edward, born in the reign of Queen Mary, nursed and weaned in the reign of Elizabeth, grew up a youth under King James, and shot up under Charles I to conquer the hierarchy—its adversary."[7]

Many of the Puritan pastors and leaders were prepared for the gospel ministry by their studies at Oxford or Cambridge. They preached the incarnate Word from the written Word with prayerful dependence on the Holy Spirit and a clear sense of purpose: that God would be glorified as people repented and believed the gospel, and then obeyed Christ in the fellowship of his church and in their daily work in the world. In all this, they were continuing the ministry of the Reformers and the Lord's apostles before them.

At that first Pentecost after Christ's resurrection, when the Holy Spirit came with power upon those praying disciples, Peter did not dwell on his experience of glossolalia but proclaimed the Lord Jesus—his humiliation and his exaltation. Peter summoned people to repentance and offered them the forgiveness of sins through the work of Christ, as well as the gift of the Spirit. Paul was also devoted to preaching Christ, particularly Christ crucified, the Saviour who paid the penalty of our sins and opened the way for us to have peace with God.

Preaching is not universally held in high esteem these days. It is often depreciated, especially by those who lack the discipline and passion to do it well. A pastor's day can be so involved in matters of secondary and even tertiary importance that the priority of preaching the Word is crowded out. Administration, visitation, counselling, and community relations have their place, but they should never rob the communication of the Word from its place of primacy. When that happens, the consequences may be catastrophic. "The days are coming," declares the Sovereign LORD, "when I will send a famine through the land—not a famine of food or a thirst for water, but a famine of hearing the words of the LORD" (Amos 8:11, NIV).

Let all who are called to feed God's flock renew their commitment to preach the Word in season and out of season, correcting, rebuking, and encouraging, with great patience and careful instruction (2 Tim. 4:2).

The Puritans provide us with a model of faithful biblical preaching. There are those who compare the multiple headings and abounding subdivisions of a typical Puritan sermon to the bones Ezekiel beheld in the valley of his vision: they were many, all very dry, and definitely quite dead. Undoubtedly, some of their homilies would have benefited from sensitive editing. But such criticisms say more about the shortness of the average listener's attention span today than they do about a Puritan pastor's supposed prolixity.

True, they produced sermons replete with introductions, expositions, clarifications, objections, exhortations, dehortations, illustrations, applications, doctrines, duties, invitations, promises, warnings and consolations. Yet we can derive lasting benefit from focusing on the insights of these biblical preachers. In studying their sermons, writings, and lectures, we will be enriched as their homiletical heritage prompts us to persevere in the reading and teaching of the inspired Scriptures.

Chapter 1

The *infallible* Word

Blessed are the seminarians who are privileged, in the providence of God, to prepare for ministry with scholars who are totally committed to the incarnate Word revealed by the Holy Spirit in the written Word. These faculty members do not take their vows with ecclesiastical tongue in ecclesiastical cheek but acknowledge their conviction that holy men of God spoke and wrote as they were moved by the Holy Spirit.

Everyone who occupies a pulpit ought also to be persuaded of the necessity, authority, clarity, and finality of God's written Word. Doubt and denial with reference to the Scriptures is bound to result in doctrinal confusion and spiritual decline. But there is a way forward—by going back to writers and preachers who were used of God in the Reformation and the Puritan era that followed.

The work of the Holy Spirit

John Owen (1616-1683) was a Puritan considered by many as "England's Calvin." In 1677, Owen's *The Reason of Faith* was a definitive answer to those who questioned why the Puritans believed the Bible to be God's inspired and infallible Word. This conviction was not based on any endorsement by the Church of Rome but on the Spirit of illumination, supplication, and consolation.[1]

Owen believed that one could come to the knowledge of God, and of his will, because the Spirit gives us a right understanding of what the Bible claims for itself. Before God's revelation was inscripturated, Satan did his worst to possess the minds of men with his delusions.[2]

We come to the knowledge of God and his will because the Spirit of inspiration is also the Spirit of illumination. In order to be enlightened by the Word, however, two things are necessary: the acceptance of Scripture as divine revelation (1 Thess. 2:13) and the study of Scripture to discover the truths taught in the Bible (Ps. 119:130). The God of truth is the object of faith. We rest on his authority and veracity; he cannot lie (Deut. 32:4); his Word is truth (John 17:17)—that is why he is worthy of trust.

Owen comments on the wonderful design of Scripture. It is given, first, to revere God to us; secondly, to direct us in the enjoyment of God.[3] Thus we may focus on what matters most: knowing God and knowing ourselves in relation to him. Those who lack such guidance grope after grotesque gods and stumble in an endless maze of uncertainties, amid darkness, ignorance, and blindness. Though Scripture dispels that darkness, some follow the false imagination of their weak and distempered minds.[4]

Owen notes that the faith whereby we believe the Scripture to be the Word of God is wrought in us by the Holy Spirit, and the Spirit produces the saving illumination of the mind—a supernatural light.[5] We should not look for external and immediate revelations, such as were granted to the prophets, apostles, and other penmen of the Scripture.[6] We seek not visions and voices from heaven but ask that the Spirit liberate our minds from darkness, ignorance, and prejudice, enabling us to discern spiritual things as we ought.[7] The internal testimony of the Spirit assures us of the divine origin and authority of the Scripture. Every supposed revelation is to be tested by Scripture.

Owen warns against an *outward* profession of the truth of Scripture divorced from an *inward* experience of its power.[8]

The Bible is not a fanatical story of madmen but divine revelation worthy of trust, written by men who have seen God's glory. We see the divine effect of the Word in the conversion of souls and sinners to God. His mighty efficacy is manifested by his power to change, convert, and renew men in the image and likeness of God.[9]

In Scripture, we have the foundation of our faith and obedience, but we cannot understand Scripture without the effectual aid and assistance of the Spirit of God. He is the only safe Guide to bring us to the full assurance of the mind and will of God. We need the opening of our understanding by an act of the power and grace of Christ, if we would understand the Scriptures.[10]

Irrational enthusiasts look for new revelations, neglecting what God has already revealed in the Scriptures. What we need, however, is an understanding of the mind of God—of all sacred truths—as revealed. This is evident in the encounter of the Ethiopian eunuch and Philip the evangelist discussing the fifty-third chapter of Isaiah's prophecy. All divine truths necessary to be known and believed, that we may live unto God in faith and obedience or come to Christ and abide in him, and all we need to be preserved from seducers is contained in Scripture.[11]

If God teaches, we are to learn. And we cannot learn except in the exercise of our minds irradiated by the Spirit. This is the way to cope with abominable errors… false worship… divisions, scandals, animosities, violence, mutual rage, and persecutions. So shall we discern and abhor every false way. We should also treat heretics with pity and compassion of their present state…and fear of their future ruin. Pray for the work of the Spirit to bring about the renovation of the mind, since he is the great Purifier and Sanctifier of the church.[12]

Let us look upon Scripture as a treasury of divine truths. Here we discover the foundation, rule, and guide of the whole church, the spiritual food and means of life to all its members.[13] Owen commends Martin Bucer (1491-1551), John Calvin (1509-1564),

Peter Martyr Vermigli (1499-1562), and Theodore Beza (1519-1605) for their great and holy works, so helpful to all who humbly seek the mind of God revealed in Scripture. Thus does the Spirit communicate to our minds a saving knowledge of God and his will, so that we may live to him and come to the enjoyment of him in his glory.[14]

The authority of the Word

From the *Works* of William Pemble (*c.*1591-1623), a learned minister of the Word, we have additional comments on the trustworthiness and authority of Holy Scripture. Pemble was a preacher who was associated with Magdalen College, Oxford. His *Works* was published posthumously in 1635. With a tongue as sharp as his pen, he denounced the errors of atheists, agnostics, Pelagians, Semi-Pelagians, Socinians, Arminians, Papists, brawling controversialists, and the gaudy gayness of anyone caught up in the malice and subtlety of that old serpent the devil. He exposed Satan as one who distracts from the truth, disseminates falsehood, and corrupts the mind with pride and self-conceit, a bastard begotten betwixt a learned head and an unsanctified heart, leading to heresy and schism.[15]

Pemble emphasized the need of believing and doing in response to biblical revelation. A Christian is one who is disciplined in the school of Christ, accepting the doctrines and duties plainly taught in Holy Scripture. The preaching of the inspired and infallible Word is of the utmost importance. Trendy sermons delivered in entertainment centres masquerading as sanctuaries have no place in Pemble's way of thinking. He deplores the sad state of affairs evident in more than a few churches, and wonders about how many discourses are tortured, wrested, pinched, obscured through hidden allusions, forced phrases, deformities of plain preaching, making the mind a slave to the tongue. He is convinced that such a "ministry" will never bring lost sheep home to the fold. Such labour requires plain speech through which the compassionate voice of the Chief Shepherd is clearly heard.[16]

Of course, a man may preach the Word faithfully and still meet with a negative response. Men may stop their ears, talk with a companion, read a book... while the minister is speaking; they may set their thoughts moving in their chests, in the brothels, in the store-houses, anywhere but where their bodies are, about anything but the sermon.[17]

Two things gain credit to the preacher of the Word: wisdom and skill that he be not deceived himself; fidelity and honesty, that he will not deceive others. People will not trust a preacher who is wise but dishonest nor a simple man even though he is honest.[18]

The preacher of the Word should not be mired in trivialities—with what Pemble calls "toys and trifles." He should expound the precepts and principles of Scripture, the historical passages dealing with the past, poetical passages such as parables and allegories, and predictions—prophecies and promises—of things to come. He should also avoid superficial flourishes of rhetorical discourse. Nothing must obscure the communication of the Word—both the law and the gospel. They have but one common end: the glory of God in man's eternal salvation.[19]

John Owen

Chapter 2

No *upstart* sect

The Protestant Reformers and their Puritan descendants were concerned to prove that they were not sectarian upstarts whose genesis was to be found in the act of a German monk and a church door in Wittenberg (i.e. Martin Luther, 1483-1546). They were sure of their continuity with the faith "once for all delivered to the saints" (Jude 3). Their lineage went through the Church Fathers to the apostles and prophets of ancient times. As mainstream evangelicals, committed to basic Christianity, they included an affirmation of the Trinity, the Decalogue, the Apostles' Creed, and the Lord's Prayer in their confessions of faith and instructive catechisms. We do well to rediscover, declare, and defend this heritage in our time.

The holy Trinity

In 1663, John Owen produced a declaration and vindication of the doctrine of the holy Trinity, accommodated to the capacity and use of such as may be in danger to be seduced, to establish the truth. He affirmed the unity of God and the divinity of the Father, the Son, and the Holy Spirit. He writes that we are confronted with what God says about himself of the Scriptures, namely, that God is One—that this one God is revealed in three Persons, distinct from each other, yet in fellowship with one another from all eternity. The Father is God.[1] The Son is God. The Spirit is God. But the Spirit is not the Father, nor is the Father the Son. Scripture reveals the Father, Son, and Holy Spirit to be one God… these are one in essence.[2] There is one God, and this God is Father, Son, and Holy Spirit.[3]

Some oppose this sacred truth and divine mystery, with disputes and cavils against the Trinity and so entangle many weak and unstable souls.[4] But the oneness of God is clearly revealed in passages such as Deuteronomy 6:4 and Isaiah 44:6-8. Scripture also teaches that there is a plurality of persons in the Deity.[5] Christ is not only human but also divine. He is to be served and worshipped on account of his own divine excellencies.[6] Consider for example Psalm 45:6. There the psalmist refers to the enthronement of the everlasting God. Yet in Hebrews 1:8, that text is definitely applied to Christ. Psalm 68:17-18 speaks of the victorious Lord, but in Ephesians 4:8-10 the passage is applied to Christ. Psalm 110:1 is clearly a reference to God, but in Matthew 22:44 it is applied to the Messiah. Or think of Isaiah 6:1-3, where mention is made of the glorious and holy God—undoubtedly applied to Christ in John 12:41. Other texts along this line are: Isaiah 9:6, John 1:1-3,14, and John 20:28. The sure and certain evidence of Christ's deity is found in Romans 1:3-4 where we read of his mighty resurrection by the power of the Holy Spirit. Christ is equal with God (Phil. 2:6), the great God who is our Saviour (Tit. 2:13-14), the God who is over all, blessed forever (Rom. 9:5).

Despite the heretical stance of Socinans, Unitarians, Jehovah's Witnesses, and liberal Protestants, the Godhead of Christ, the eternal Son of God, is unequivocally declared and defended by all who take the Scriptures seriously.

The deity and personality of the Holy Spirit are also revealed in the Word. He is the object of our faith, worship, and obedience.[7] His "divine operations" include the regeneration, sanctification, consolation, and glorification of God's elect.

We are baptized in the name of this triune God (Matt. 28:19), and, to be a temple of the Holy Spirit is nothing less than being indwelt by God (1 Cor. 3:16).

The Decalogue

One Puritan edition of the Decalogue reads like this on its title page:

> The
> Law Unsealed
> Or, a Practical
> Exposition
> Of the
> Ten Commandments
> With
> A resolution of several
> Momentous Questions and
> Cases of Conscience.
>
> By the Learned, Laborious,
> Faithful Servant of Jesus Christ,
> Mr. James Durham, late
> Minister of the Gospel
> At Glasgow.
> Edinburgh, 1676

James Durham's (1622-1658) exposition was prefaced by commendatory epistles from John Owen and William Jenkyn (*bap.* 1613-1685). Commenting on Exodus 20, Durham underlines the fact that the God who mercifully and mightily liberated Israel from slavery in Egypt is also the God who speaks. Let the people express their gratitude to him by obeying his commandments given to them through Moses. The breach of the holy law of God is no less sinful to us now than it was to them before us.[8] God's moral law must be both preached and practiced. We should never forget that the great motive of our obedience... is not fear of threatenings and wrath in case of disobedience... but love and gratitude, not simply to God as Creator but as Redeemer.[9]

This law was given in two tables. The first relates to the duties we owe God, and the second concerns our obligations to one another in family, church, and society. All the commandments come with divine authority. We should be careful to note what each of them forbids and commands.

We must not have any other gods on the altar of the heart (Exod. 20:3). God alone, revealed in the Father, Son, and Holy Spirit, is the focus of our worship. Idolatry is the root of all sin, since it displaces God with someone or something that usurps the allegiance and affection we owe to him alone (Exod. 20:4-6). Do not profane but rather revere God's holy name (Exod. 20:7). Observe one day in seven for rest and worship (Exod. 20:8-11). This includes prayer... praise... preaching... hearing... and receiving sacraments[10] as well as works of mercy and works of necessity.[11]

The second table of the law begins with a command regarding the honour we owe to our parents (Exod. 20:12). This precept is linked to a promise designed to encourage obedience (Eph. 6:2). The sixth commandment forbids wilful, malicious, and premeditated homicide as well as passion, hatred, and anger (Exod. 20:13). The seventh commandment does more than forbid adultery (Exod. 20:14). It prohibits all that would hinder our sanctification of body no less than soul or spirit (1 Thess. 4:3-7). God has not called us to moral uncleanness but to holiness (Eph. 5:3-5). We cannot grow in holiness while cultivating the works of the flesh (Gal. 5:19-21). Durham discusses adultery, fornication, drunkenness, gluttony, and cosmetics in expounding this commandment. Yet, he somehow omits any reference to the positive aspects of it, namely, that the expression of human sexuality in a lifelong monogamous relationship between husband and wife is not only permitted but blest of God (Gen. 2:18-25; Eph. 5:22-33).

Robbery, plunder, piracy, and misappropriation are violations of the eighth commandment (Exod. 20:15). So also are biting usury and defrauding creditors.[12] Let us rather provide for ourselves, our families, and others in need (1 Tim. 5:8; Neh. 5:14). Next, bearing false witness is prohibited, especially before judges (Exod. 20:16; Col. 3:9; Eph. 4:25). Included are whispering, tale bearing, prevarication, and the tattling of busybodies.[13] Finally, we are warned about the sin of covetousness or greed (Exod. 20:17). This is the attitude that leads to false witness, theft, adultery, and even murder.

The Apostles' Creed

William Perkins (1558-1602) studied at Christ's College, Cambridge, was a prolific commentator on Scripture, and was also knowledgable in Patristics, Roman Catholicism, witchcraft, and astrology. His works, published posthumously in 1603, include *An Exposition of the Symbole or Creed of the Apostles*.[14]

At the very outset, Perkins affirms that faith is wrought by the ministry of the Word and the work of the Spirit, who enlightens the mind and moves the will:

> I believe in God the Father Almighty, personally putting my whole trust in him. Such faith brings consolation and comfort. God is called "Father" because we are regenerated by him, and adopted into his family through the merit of Christ.
>
> I believe in Jesus Christ. From the fall of Adam springs original sin, which then produces actual sin—the fruit of a corrupt heart in thought, will and deed. From sin, only Christ can set us free. Jesus is both a perfect and absolute Saviour (Matt. 1:21; Acts 4:12). He delivers us from the guilt and punishment of our sins, when we see ourselves as lost and put our trust in him. Christ, by his incarnation, came down from heaven to us, that we being partakers of his grace might ascend up to heaven by him. As man, he has no father. As God, he has no mother.
>
> By reason of our sins, we are God's debtors, bankrupt

before him, yet the Son of God became our surety and was crucified to discharge our debt.

There is a quickening virtue in the resurrection of Christ, whereby he is not only able to raise our dead bodies to life, but also when we are dead in sin to raise us up to newness of life. He shall come to judge the living and the dead.

I believe in the Holy Spirit, the third person of the Godhead. He is my sanctifier and strengthener. He indwells the elect, the temple of the Holy Spirit. If we live in the Spirit, we will die to sin and produce the fruit of the Spirit.

The holy catholic church is the company of all who are predestined to life everlasting. Predestination is a part of the counsel of God, whereby he has before all times purposed in himself to show mercy on some, and pass by others to show his justice, manifesting the glory of his name. We must give all diligence to make our calling and election sure (2 Peter 1:8-11). We believe in the communion of saints—not dead men listed in the pope's calendar, but all who are sanctified by the blood of Christ. We believe in the forgiveness of sins, for the sake of Christ; the resurrection of the body, and the life everlasting. So, the Church of Rome has no cause to condemn us as heretics since we truly hold and believe the whole Apostles' Creed, which is an epitome of the Scriptures and the very key of faith.

The Lord's Prayer

The *Shorter Catechism* produced by the Westminster Assembly in 1647, defines prayer as an offering up of our desires unto God, for things agreeable to his will, in the name of Christ, with confession of our sins and thankful acknowledgment of his mercies.

Christ has given his disciples a pattern for prayer, commonly called The Lord's Prayer. Its preface teaches us to approach God with reverence and confidence. In the first petition, "Hallowed be Thy name," we pray that God would enable us and others to glorify him in all that whereby he makes himself known, and that he would dispose all things to his own glory. In the second petition, "Thy kingdom come," we pray that Satan's kingdom may be destroyed, and that the kingdom of grace may be advanced, ourselves and others brought into it, and kept in it, and that the kingdom of glory may be hastened. In the third petition, "Thy will be done on earth as it is in heaven," we pray that God by his grace would make us able and willing to know, obey, and submit to his will in all things, as the angels do in heaven.

After the priority of prayer related to God's name, kingdom, and will, we pray for our own needs. In the fourth petition, "Give us this day our daily bread," we pray that of God's free gift we may receive a competent portion of the good things of this life and enjoy his blessing with them. In the fifth petition, which is, "And forgive us our debts as we forgive our debtors," we pray that God, for Christ's sake, would freely pardon all our sins; which we are the rather encouraged to ask, because by his grace we are enabled from the heart to forgive others. In the sixth petition, which is, "And lead us not into temptation, but deliver us from evil," we pray that God would either keep us from being tempted to sin, or support and deliver us when we are tempted. To him do we ascribe kingdom, power, and glory and in testimony of our desire, and assurance to be heard, we say, Amen.[15]

Thomas Watson

Chapter 3

The *Messiah* revealed

John Owen's catechisms, designed for the instruction of his congregations, were first published in 1645. The *Lesser Catechism* was prepared for children, and the *Greater* for adults. It is a sad commentary on the doctrinal knowledge of more than a few church members to note that many of them would find it difficult to define their answers clearly and coherently if faced with the questions of that *Lesser Catechism* today.

Jesus the Messiah is presented as the One consecrated or anointed to be the Redeemer of God's elect. We suffer from a triple problem: ignorance, iniquity, and mortality. But Jesus the Christ deals decisively with our predicament. As the supreme Prophet, he deals with our ignorance. As the merciful High Priest, he atones for our iniquity and intercedes for us in heaven. As the righteous King, he defeats death, and brings life and immortality to light.

Our Lord's exercise of his messianic ministry was prepared by his incarnation. He was conceived by the Holy Spirit and born of the virgin Mary. To his eternal deity was added a perfect humanity. Thus related to the Father and to us, he was admirably suited to serve as Mediator and Reconciler. He is the Way, the True Way and the Living Way. No one comes to the Father but by Jesus

Christ, who came from the Father (John 14:6). Through him, the invisible God is revealed. With eyes of faith, we may behold his glory, the glory of the Son who came from the Father, full of grace and truth. He is the radiance of God's glory, the exact representation of his being (John 1:14; Heb. 1:3).

Enlightened by a revelation from heaven, the apostle Peter recognized Jesus as the Christ, the Son of the living God. He is the consecrated and Anointed One, the Christ, the Messiah, sent to be our Prophet, Priest, and King. As long as the church makes this confession with integrity, it will stand firmly on solid rock and the gates of hell will not overcome it (Matt. 16:13-18).

The Puritans dealt with many theological and ethical subjects, but they were particularly Christ-centred in their preaching and writing.

Prophet, Priest, and King

Thomas Watson (c.1620-1686), like many other Puritans, refused to comply with the demands of royal absolution and so was ejected from his parish in 1662. Among his sermons and writings are several that expound the redemptive work of Jesus Christ.

After defining sin as a lack of conformity to, or a transgression of, the law of God, involving corruption and deserving condemnation, Watson goes on to describe the person and work of Jesus the Messiah. If the bad news is sin and judgement, the good news is that God did not leave all mankind to perish in its condition of sin and misery. Instead, he entered into a covenant of grace to liberate his elect out of that state and bring them into a state of grace by means of a Redeemer. Jesus is the Mediator of this new covenant. Contrary to the heresy of syncretism, "salvation is found in no one else, for there is no other name under heaven given to men by which we must be saved" (Acts 4:12, NIV).

In the unique person of Christ, there are two natures—one human, the other divine—constituting a veritable bridge of reconciliation between a holy God and a penitent people.[1]

Jesus is the supreme Prophet promised in Deuteronomy 18:15.

As the Spirit speaks to us in the Scriptures, this infallible Prophet instructs us; he opens our understanding; his Word is a lamp to our feet and a light to our path (Ps. 119:105; John 16:13-14). He deals decisively with our ignorance, dispelling our darkness. He gives us a spirit of discernment, with the light of truth (John 8:12). Others may instruct, but cannot command obedience… When he comes to teach, he remedies obstinacy and inclines the will to be willing. When he teaches us, we are moved to learn, while fools despise instruction.[2]

Watson encourages us to choose Christ as our Prophet. Otherwise, we shall never be wise to salvation. What shall we do to have him for our teacher? We must see our need of his teaching and turn to him for instruction (Rev. 3:18; Ps. 25:5).

In his ministry, Jesus not only healed diseases but preached and taught (Matt. 4:23). He assumed the prophetic office that he might give us knowledge. Let us, then, go to Christ for teaching and wait upon the means of grace, which he has appointed for our good. As we live according to the knowledge and understanding we already possess, he will show us more.[3]

As John Flavel (*c.*1628-1691), another Puritan, put it: "Christ came to expound the Law and reveal God's will. When God's will is known and understood, we have no freedom of choice but are bound by it—be God's command ever so difficult to obey, or the sin it forbids ever so tempting."[4]

Flavel continues: "Christ was a very plain preacher, clothing sublime and spiritual mysteries in earthly metaphors. Now he would have his ministers use great plainness of speech. He would rather have them pierce people's ears than amuse their fancies. Christ commands his ministers to preserve the simplicity and purity of the gospel, and not to blend and sophisticate it."[5]

Richard Sibbes (1577-1635) pointed his hearers to listen to Jesus, "the prophet beyond all others, who can instruct the soul…open the understanding, and use the key of the heart which can open the soul."[6]

Thomas Watson reminds his readers that we are obliged to Jesus

Christ, the great Prophet, for opening to us the eternal purposes of his love and revealing to us the mysteries of the kingdom of heaven.[7]

In discussing the priestly office of Jesus, Watson quotes from the *Westminster Shorter Catechism*: Christ executes the office of a priest in his once offering up of himself a sacrifice to satisfy divine justice, and reconciling us to God, and in making continual intercession for us (Heb. 9:26). This involved his *active* obedience (doing the Father's will with perfect and willing compliance) and his *passive* obedience (paying the penalty deserved by the sins of his people). Christ was not only a Lamb without spot, but a Lamb slain.[8]

Christ mediates between a holy God and guilty sinners. By our sins, we had infinitely wronged God. We could never have pacified an angry deity. Therefore, God's justice can only be satisfied by the sacrifice of Christ. Thus did Jesus fulfil the predictions of Scripture and bring us back into favour with God. As Augustine put it, "The cross was a pulpit from which Christ preached his love to the world. O infinite, amazing, love of Christ!"[9]

The sacrifice of Christ is the blood of atonement. Now, having entered into heaven, Christ intercedes for us. Exalted to glory, yet he is compassionately mindful of his people on earth. He is holy (Heb. 7:26), faithful (Heb. 2:17), immortal (Heb. 7:25), interceding for the elect—for even the weakest believers.[10] Christ, our great High Priest, does three things: he presents the merit of his sacrifice to his Father and, in virtue of the price he paid, pleads for mercy; by his intercession, he answers every charge brought against his elect; and by his intercession, he calls for acquittal, as our Advocate (Lev. 16:11-16; Rom. 8:33; 1 John 2:1). His affectionate pleading is efficacious and prevailing.[11] Let us, therefore, approach the throne of grace with boldness, and look confidently for absolutism at the day of judgement (Heb. 4:16, John 5:22).[12]

We come now to consider Jesus Christ in his kingly office. Flavel notes that what Jesus revealed as a Prophet, he purchased as a Priest; what he revealed and purchased as a Prophet and Priest, he applies as King: first, by subduing the souls of his people to his spiritual government, and then by ruling them as his subjects, ordering all things in the kingdom of his providence for their good. Christ exercises a kingly power over the souls of all whom the gospel subdues to his obedience. And he obtains a throne in the hearts of men by conquest, sending forth his armies of prophets, evangelists, pastors, and teachers, under the leading of the Spirit, armed with that two-edged sword, the Word of God.[13]

Watson rejoices in the regal office of Christ, who is King of kings and Lord of lords (Rev. 19:16). He rules his people by authority and affection. As King, he makes laws; and by his laws, he rules. He also rules by love, full of mercy and clemency. He offers promises as well as precepts. This King is comparable to a lion and also a lamb. He will reward his subjects with inner peace and joy but will also vanquish all the enemies of his church. He is the King crowned with many crowns. As Myconius wrote in a letter to Calvin, "I am glad Christ reigns, else I should have despaired."[14]

Of Christ the King, Watson says, "He subdues things unconquerable… and conquers the world, death, hell, and sin—all things that are terrible… He rules over the soul and conscience… guides our thoughts, desires, actions, and affections, setting up a peaceable government."[15]

Watson concludes, "If you are a subject of Christ, you are sure to reign with Christ forever."[16]

Richard Baxter

Chapter 4

Pastoral ministry

In 1656, Richard Baxter (1615-1691) published *The Reformed Pastor*, a book destined to bring guidance and encouragement to generations of pastors. It is based on Acts 20:28, where the apostle Paul exhorts the leaders of the Ephesian congregation to keep watch over themselves and all the flock of which the Holy Spirit had made them overseers. They are called to be shepherds of the church of God, which he bought with his own blood.

This same emphasis is made by William Gouge (1575-1653), who shared in the work of the Westminster Assembly of Divines. After expounding the passage dealing with the whole armour of God (Eph. 6:10-17), so that Christians may defeat the devil and defend the faith, the apostle asks believers to pray not just for all of God's people but especially and particularly for those called to the ministry of the gospel (Eph. 6:18-20). The things Gouge draws out of this Scripture are as relevant now as they were then.

Gouge on the ministry

Paul was, by virtue of his calling a minister of the gospel and a public minister to the whole world, by reason of his apostleship.

Through a powerful and effectual ministry, he planted churches. Ephesus was one of these, so that he was considered the spiritual father of that people... As a minister of the gospel, he requests prayer for himself, that he might have liberty to preach that gospel. The Ephesians are to be particularly mindful of their ministers in their prayer to God.

Why pray for them? First, their calling is the most excellent, necessary, and profitable, having to do with the spiritual, heavenly, and eternal God of both body and soul. Second, of all callings, the ministry is the most difficult. The apostle wonders, "Who is sufficient for these things?"[1]

Consider the pastoral work itself: to quicken such as are dead in sin; to raise up and restore the fallen; to comfort the troubled in conscience; to strengthen the weak; to encourage the faint-hearted; to confound the obstinate; to stand against all adverse powers... remember that they are only flesh and blood, subject to the same passions as others.

Faithful ministers are most opposed by Satan and his instruments. As the scribes, Pharisees, Sadducees, and Herodians persecuted Christ, so those engaged in their ministerial labours have to face such foes... Satan knows that the sheep will soon scatter if the shepherd is smitten... If they perish, many perish with them.

Therefore, pray for ministers. Pray that the Lord will send forth faithful labourers. Forget not your pastors. You know the benefit of faithful preaching and your need of it. Therefore, pray for them.[2]

What should you pray for on behalf of ministers? And why? Pray that they may proclaim the gospel clearly, making known its mystery with liberty of speech. Treat them as ambassadors of the gospel... Remember that they have no ability to perform their ministerial functions unless it be given them. Without Christ, they can do nothing (John 15:5). Their sufficiency comes from him alone.

Paul took great pains to fulfil his ministry properly, but he did so by the grace of God. One may plant and another water, but

God alone gives the increase. Pray that they may speak his Word with boldness (Acts 4:29).

The ministry was appointed to gather the people together, to bring them to the unity of faith, to lead them to a knowledge of the Son of God. Pray that they may have the ability to do his work.[3]

Some seek places of dignity, others desire applause and the praise of men... These are things men hunt after... But how many wish that their ministers should be able, faithful, and careful? Do they really want ministers who examine what knowledge, faith, repentance, and other such graces you may have? Let such as respect God's glory, the edification of his church, or the salvation of their own souls learn what to pray for on their minister's behalf.

Pray for freedom of utterance. There is a message to deliver. The ability to speak well, without sound content, is mere vanity. It can only tickle the hearer's ears. Ministers must be apt to teach (1 Tim. 3:2), having something worth saying and saying it well.[4]

Little regard have they for the good of God's church, who spend all their days at the university, or in some such place of learning, to gather more and more knowledge and understanding of divinity, but never exercise themselves in utterance. They never preach and never pray. Though they may know much, yet their people are not at all edified.[5]

Then there are those who fleece the flock but feed it not. They drive away many from our churches... They do good to none but bring much hurt to many.

Even the gifted need prayer, lest they trust to themselves and proceed without the help of others... God will justly punish the pride of such ministers.

Ministers should cultivate a plain, distinct, audible delivery... They should avoid speaking in whispers between the teeth and lips, as though they were afraid of being heard... Like the prophets who were commanded to cry aloud, ministers should utter the Word so that it may be heard distinctly and audibly... Else people are deprived of the benefit of the message.

If one should come upon a stage and could not be heard, he

would be hissed off. Why then should such come into a pulpit?[6]

Some, however, fall into another extreme: needless clamour... As in other things, so in this also: a good mean and moderation, guided with judgement and discretion, is to be used.

The manner of utterance is boldness, opposed to an evil, unseemly fearfulness. This implies a holy courage and liberty, which a minister takes to himself, remembering the Master who sent him and the office deputed to him... undaunted by the persons of men and all their contradictions and oppositions... Boldness, courage, and freedom of speech are needful for a minister in the execution of his ministry (Jer. 1:17; Ezek. 2:6). Christ manifested great boldness in his ministry, for he taught as one having authority [Matt. 7:29]. His hearers were astonished. This boldness made him freely to rebuke the scribes and Pharisees, uncovering both the errors of their doctrine and the corruptions of their life. Such was the boldness of his forerunner, John the Baptist. Great was the boldness of the apostles (Acts 4:13).

Many people are imprudent, stiff-necked, fierce, and violent... We see, by common experience, how everyone will trample on him who is fearful and faint-hearted... People will tread on the timorous. But if a minister is bold, a man of courage who freely declares his message, he will dismay his proudest enemies.[7]

This boldness is to be manifested by an impartial preaching of the Word, without respect of persons... by a declaration of the whole truth of God... by a grave, plain, free delivery of God's Word, without affectation... by reproving sin with authority, so that transgressors may be brought to shame... by despising all fear of reproach... with fear... but with wisdom and courage.[8]

The minister is to make known the mystery of the gospel and so edify the church, the body of Christ... All the understanding of the gospel which God gives to ministers is a talent given them to occupy and employ by making known what they know... Take heed, O ministers, that you be not as covetous worldlings, who are ever gathering but never spend—like the unprofitable servant... Let us not, through negligence, conceal our knowledge and prove unprofitable (Matt. 25:14-30).

The gospel is the proper object of preaching. Christ gave his disciples a commission to preach the gospel... The goal of preaching is the salvation of men's souls... The gospel is the power of God unto salvation (Rom. 1:16). If this is not the object of preaching, then the main and principal end has been missed.[9]

The law also is to be preached, but as a preparative to the gospel... it is God's schoolmaster to bring us to Christ. What is the mystery of the gospel? It is a divine secret, containing things which eye has not seen, nor ear heard, nor have come into man's heart [1 Cor. 2:9]... known by divine revelation.[10]

The gospel was never written in man's nature. It was extraordinarily revealed and must not now be lightly and slightly passed over. It requires our best study and meditation... and prayer to God, that he may give us the Spirit of illumination... Let us, therefore, have recourse to God's Word where this mystery is revealed; let us pray to God by his Spirit to reveal it to us.

The apostle's role was that of an ambassador of the gospel: to declare and make known the gospel... God will require a particular account of that particular function to which he appoints any man... Endeavour, therefore, to labour after and pray for the preaching of the gospel in a manner acceptable to God... Let our calling be always in our minds, remembering that we are God's stewards, dispensers of the mysteries of God, ministers of Jesus Christ, God's labourers, planters, waterers, builders, bishops, pastors, watchmen, ambassadors...

Ministers are called to be ambassadors of the Word, representing Christ—the great Lord and King—offering reconciliation to the world and preaching the glad tidings of salvation. This metaphor and title (ambassador) being applied to the ministerial function, sets forth three things: the dignity of the ministry, the duties of ministers, [and] the mercy of God in ordaining them to their function.[11]

Let people learn from this how to respect ministers... diligently attending to our message, willing to follow our instructions, esteeming us as God's messengers and Christ's representatives. Therefore, men must look not on our persons (for we are not better than others) but on our ministry and message (for therein we excel all others.) The honour and good which in this respect is done to us, Christ accounts as done to himself.

Those who reproach or disgrace our calling, or abuse our persons for our office's sake, they reproach and abuse our Master (Luke 10:16). Can such despisers of God's ministers think they shall escape just vengeance (Matt. 10:14-15)?[12]

The duties which are required of ministers in virtue of their ambassage are two. First, to carry themselves worthy of the dignity and excellency of their positions: very circumspect, sober, honourable, wise. So ought ministers of the Word to behave themselves as becomes the ambassadors of the great Lord of heaven (Col. 1:10; Phil. 1:27). Second, to be faithful in delivering their message. This faithfulness consists in three special points:

1. In delivering nothing but what he has received of his Master and is agreeable to his will (Matt. 28:18-19).
2. In not being moved by fear or favour, when delivering his Master's message.
3. In delivering God's Word as the Word of God (1 Peter 4:11).[13]

That God's Word may be thus delivered, several requirements must be met. First, gravity—opposed to lightness and vain affectation. A wise ambassador will not deliver his message like a stage-player or a child lacking in seriousness. Second, he will present his message with authority, without fear, but accompanied by divine power and with an admirable majesty (Tit. 2:15). Deliver God's Word in his name, with the authority he as committed to you, so that the message may be received as the Word of God (1 Thess. 2:13). Third, [present it with] sincerity, as opposed to falsifying or adulterating the Word of God. Deliver the message pure and sincere, nourishing all who hear.[14]

This excellent and high calling is not committed to ministers for their own sakes, for their honour and reknown, to exalt them or puff them up. This calling requires diligence, so that they are described as workmen, labourers, watchmen, shepherds, servants, ambassadors, ministers, and stewards. God has manifested his great mercy to his church in appointing men to be his ambassadors on earth who will declare his will to his people.[15]

In Christ's stead, and in his name, ministers are to preach peace and offer reconciliation. A private man may have great knowledge of the mystery of the gospel and be able to open and declare its sense and meaning, but a minister—by virtue of his office—has this prerogative and preeminence above others, that in God's stead he declares reconciliation. When a minister preaches and applies the promise of the gospel, he not only declares and makes known God's mercy and goodness to sinners but may move them to believe those promises and to embrace reconciliation with God. Isn't this a strong prop to our faith, and doesn't this bring great comfort and peace to distressed souls?

Reject not the offer of peace made by God's ambassadors just because they are mere men. Yield not to Satan's suggestions. Rather, receive them as God's messengers and Christ's representatives. Receive the Word preached by them as God's Word. Whoever esteems lightly this ministry, and believes not their messages, turns away from the very Word of God and judges himself unworthy of eternal life (Acts 13:46).[16]

If, for the sins of England, God should deprive us of the light of the gospel and of our Christian magistrates, and give us over to the power of adversaries... let us not think ourselves, our brothers, or the gospel, disgraced, and thus be ashamed of our profession... Scripture makes such persecution a matter of honour and rejoicing (Acts 5:41).[17]

The apostles were persecuted for preaching the gospel, and others for believing the gospel. They suffered for preaching or professing the doctrine of Christ... But those who suffer for Christ will also reign with Christ (2 Tim. 2:12).[18]

When and where it pleases God to raise up Christian magistrates who love the gospel and defend the gospel, its ambassadors are kept from public persecution. Yet the greater sort of people will privately scorn them and wrong them... because of their message, and of their Master. The message is as contrary to the disposition of the world as can be, causing the unregenerate to fret and fume, rage and rave against it. The minister's Master is a great King, but his kingdom is not of this world.[19]

The Holy Ghost repeats not things in vain... What Scripture urges again and again we must not lightly pass over but give it more diligent heed. Pray that ministers may have boldness and freedom of speech... proclaiming the gospel of the grace of God and finishing their course with joy (Acts 20:24). Paul was determined to finish the ministry he had received from the Lord Jesus. Persecutors chained his body, but they could not chain God's Word. Under the cross, he did not desire to have that cross removed but wanted rather to preach boldly. Such a desire demonstrates a great zeal for God's glory, the progress of the gospel, and the edification of the church. All this he prefers, before his own ease, liberty, and life itself.[20]

Pray for God's faithful ambassadors, that the Lord may grant them all boldness to speak his Word, so that his name may be the more glorified and his church edified.[21]

Owen on the ministry

In the autumn of 1673, John Owen preached a sermon on Micah 7:14 in which he emphasized the role of pastoral ministry at a time of crisis. Devastation, desolation, and destruction loomed on the horizon for both church and nation. Owen pleaded for the conversion of people to God as the one way out. He deplored the ruin of relationships, the breakdown of family life, and the apostasy that convulsed the country. Yet he believed that God would deliver his people through a caring and authoritative pastoral ministry. Through the faithful preaching of the Word, God's elect would come to saving faith. They were not only chosen by God but redeemed by Christ.[22]

On another occasion, Owen underlined the role of the Holy Spirit in ministerial endowments. The Spirit gives gifts to pastors called to serve the church and glorify the Lord. The ministry of the gospel is the ministry of the Spirit (John 14:16; 2 Cor. 3:6-8). Pastors ought to preach both the law that condemns transgressors and the gospel that quickens those who hear the Word with the hearing of faith. Ministers must address their own hearts before preaching the Word to others, rightly dividing or applying the truth of God. The pastor must know not only his text but also his people.[23]

At an ordination service on September 8, 1682, Owen urged pastors to feed God's people with knowledge and understanding. He reminded them that the ministry was no sinecure. It involved considerable effort, like that of a long-distance runner or a determined wrestler. Pastoral service demands spiritual wisdom, the proclamation of the whole counsel of God, the right use of the Spirit's gifts, and the experience of what is expounded (Acts 20:27; Eph. 1:17-18; Matt. 7:29).[24]

It is an easier thing to bring our heads to preach than our hearts to preach... To bring our heads to preach is but to fill our minds and memories with some notions of truth... But to bring our hearts to preach is to be transformed by the power of these truths... with zeal for God and compassion to the souls of men.[25]

We are to pray for the presence of Christ in all our assemblies, for on this depends all the efficacy of the ordinance of the gospel... It is incumbent on pastors and teachers of churches to preserve the truth and doctrine of the gospel—to keep it entire and defend it against all opposition (1 Tim. 6:20). We shall never contend earnestly for the truth... unless our love and value of it arise from a sense and experience of it in our own souls. One duty more is required of pastors and teachers in the church: that we labour diligently for the conversion of souls... calling and gathering the elect in all ages by [our] ministry... The first object of the Word is the world.[26]

There is a greater glory in giving a minister to a poor congregation than there is in the installment and enthronement of all the popes and cardinals and metropolitans that ever were in the world.[27]

Chapter 5

Guilt *and* grace

A rthur Hildersam (1563-1632) prepared for the gospel ministry at Christ's College, Cambridge. Disinherited for refusing to adopt Roman Catholicism, he eventually became vicar of a congregation at Ashby-de-la-Zouch in Leicestershire. Despite being threatened, silenced, restored, suspended, imprisoned, released, he never deviated from his purpose: to see people converted to Christ as Lord and Saviour. Among his writings are: *CVIII lectures upon the fourth of John*, published in London in 1656, and *CLII lectures upon Psalme LI*, published in London in 1642. His exposition of that penitential psalm runs to 735 pages and covers only the first seven verses. No one can reasonably accuse this Puritan preacher of superficiality in expounding Scripture!

An exposition of Psalm 51

Psalm 51 contains words like mercy, love, compassion, transgression, iniquity, sin, evil, truth, wisdom, joy, purity, renewal, restoration, guilt, praise, and sacrifice. These terms are not pale abstractions, but meaningful words expressive of human experience and divine grace.

The title of this psalm reflects the fact that they had music in the days of King David, with instruments and Levites edifying the people and glorifying the Lord. Hildersam notes that the singing of psalms revived the heart, made worshippers cheerful and stirred up spiritual affection. The tongue, given to glorify God, can be abused to use unclean speech that corrupts the heart and sets it on fire with filthy lust.

The sins of David were not committed by him in the heat of his youth… nor by one before his conversion, nor by a novice in religion… but by a man who had attained to a rare degree of knowledge—a regenerate man, upright in heart. A man who is truly regenerate may fall fearfully into most odious sins, yet the regenerate cannot fall finally—he shall be restored and renewed again by repentance. The use of this doctrine is not to give anyone encouragement to security in any sin, or to think: "It is no big matter for a man to slip into sin now and then, into adultery, or drunkenness, or oppression, or revenge. Even the best have their faults." No, other men's falls are recorded in Scripture to warn us, lest we do the same. We may prevent such falls, first, by nourishing in our hearts the fear of sinning against God; secondly, by dealing conscientiously with even the least of sins; thirdly, by not neglecting the means of grace; fourthly, by praying daily for God's support.[1]

So long as David lay like a swine, sleeping and snorting in that filthy puddle into which he had fallen, he could not rise or recover himself by repentance… The longer you continue in any sin, the harder will your heart become. This is a divine judgement greatly to be feared.[2]

It is no small fault to be an unprofitable hearer of God's Word… Listen with a free heart, laying aside all worldly cares and distracting thoughts… Come with a humble heart… resolved to obey whatsoever God shall teach or command you. Pray before you hear, for the preacher as well as yourself.[3]

If ministers of the gospel would do good, they must apply their doctrine to their hearers and boldly reprove their sins… He who would do the work of ministry faithfully needs to know his people well... He must also be of an unblameable life... No one can reprove sin in others who does not fear and hate sin in himself... He needs to love his people well, else his reproof will never do them good.[4]

Psalm 51 is a prayer of David, consisting of two petitions: the first concerns his justification, the forgiveness of his sins, and the imputation of Christ's righteousness to him; the second, of his sanctification, the mortifying of his corruption, and the renewing of his heart by the Spirit of God.[5]

In Psalm 51:1-2 we have the sum and effect of David's first petition... He pleads nothing but mercy. If we would turn to God by prayer, we should remove four impediments to prayer: i – the extremity of our affliction; ii – the sense of our unworthiness; iii – our inability to fulfil this duty; iv – the little good we seem to have received by it.[6]

David does not so much desire the removal of God's heavy judgements as he does the pardon of his sins. We say that Jesus shall save his people. From what? From poverty, sickness, shame, or persecution? No, from their sins (Matt. 1:21). Sin is the greatest misery and evil from which a man can be saved or delivered... David's sins do so trouble him that he cries out to God to blot them out of the debt-book. David also compares his sin to filthiness from which he needs to be cleansed. Sin pollutes and poisons everything—health, wealth, friends, children, even God's Word and sacraments.[7]

If a man feels himself to be sanctified and changed by the Spirit of Christ, then he may be sure that he is justified and washed from his sins by the blood of Christ.[8]

The Lord exacted and received by Christ's passive obedience (suffering and sacrifice) the whole forfeiture of our obligation he had against us, and so we came to the pardon of our sins... He also exacted and received in Christ's active obedience (fulfilling all righteousness) the whole debt of obedience to his law that we owed him.

Whatsoever doctrine is brought you, whether it be old Pelagianism or new popery or Semi-Pelagianism—if it derogate in the least from the glory of God's grace and ascribe anything to man—detest it, abhor it, as being an adversary to the grace of God.[9]

The secure sinner... has more need to hear the terrors of the law than the comforts of the gospel... God revealed in his Word that he does not desire nor take pleasure in the destruction of the wicked... He earnestly desires the repentance and salvation of the most wicked.[10]

Resolve within yourself that you will believe and rest upon what God has said in his Word, though a thousand devils and your own heart also should say something to the contrary when you have no feeling or comfort at all in the assurance of his favour... Rest on God's Word and promise... We live by our faith and not by our feeling... Unbelief makes us vulnerable to every temptation... Trust in God, and be persuaded of his love.[11]

In times of spiritual desertion, take the help of some faithful friend or minister with whom you may discuss your situation... It is not safe to smother and hold in such grief too long... Seek God by fervent prayer and depend on him for the recovery of your comfort... Meditate on his mercy and goodness... doubt not that he loves you.[12]

In Psalm 51:3, several things should be observed: i – that David confesses his transgressions, hiding nothing of his sins; ii – that David was moved to do this because he could not forget his sins; iii – that David is encouraged to seek mercy and pardon from the promises of God. Note also that David confessed his sin to Nathan (2 Sam. 12:13), to the people of God, and to the Lord himself. Those whose sins God has brought to light, whose sins are public and notorious, scandalous, and offensive... ought to be willing to confess their sins publicly, to make their repentance as public and notorious as their sin.[13]

Confession must be made, not in the ears of a priest but to God. Remember his promise to show mercy to those who do so. But how do we obtain this grace? In five ways: i – by knowing and understanding God's Word, without which we cannot know what sin is; ii – by discerning if we please God or not; iii – by taking an account of ourselves daily; iv – by calling past sins to remembrance; v – by asking God's help to confess your sins aright. So, go to God not as a felon to his judge but as a sick man to his physician.[14]

In Psalm 51:4-6 David confesses his sin, acknowledging the person against whom he had sinned, the source from whence this sin came, and the grace he had experienced in past times.

We must never forget that every sin is an offense against the majesty of almighty God, a contempt done to him, and a despising of his commandments. Till a man be soundly humbled for his sin, he can never thoroughly acknowledge sin [and] he can never thoroughly acknowledge [God's] righteousness in correcting him.

Only when we are assured of our peace and reconciliation with God, wrought by the gospel, will we be prepared to follow Christ through thick and thin.[15]

David tells of iniquity and sin in connection with his conception and birth. For his parents to beget him was not sinful. Marriage is an honourable estate (Heb. 13:4). But it is his own sinfulness, from the beginning, that David confesses.

Parents should be careful to maintain that authority and pre-eminence which God has given them... They should teach [their children] to know God, to know what is good, and what is evil... acquaint them with the practice of religion (the reading of the Word, prayer, the giving of thanks, and public worship) ... and give them a good example. Without this, neither your commandments nor corrections nor instructions will do them any good.[16]

The love of God is the root of all true obedience... and the evidence of saving grace within. True saving knowledge is the principal work of God's grace in the conversion of a man... It is both the foundation and seed of all other saving graces.[17]

Ministers must make it their first and chief care to bring people to knowledge... by catechizing as well as preaching... teaching plainly, so that the people may understand... studying and taking pains with our sermons.[18]

It is of God alone that the means of grace become effectual to the conversion of anyone... Conversion is wholly to be ascribed to the grace of God, and all the glory of man's salvation belongs to him alone... Although our salvation was not free to Christ, since he paid for it dearly, yet to us it is free. We obtain it only through the free grace and mercy of God.[19]

The Spirit never disagrees with the Word. He instructs the conscience by the ministry of the Word, in God's church, not by immediate inspirations and (fanatical) enthusiasms.

We are bound to rejoice in the liberty of the gospel and grieve to see it hindered or interrupted in any way. Whoever loves the church and the land he lives in with sincerity, must desire and rejoice to see the gospel freely preached in it, to see God's pure religion professed in it... Nothing else will make a nation so honourable and full of glory, so strong and peaceable, so prosperous and plentiful in all outward blessings.[20]

Chapter 6

The *second* birth

The phrase "born again" is sometimes understood—or misunderstood—in a variety of ways. Some suggest that the performance of a ritual guarantees a second birth. Others insist that regeneration involves adherence to man-made regulations, which are neither commanded nor condemned by Scripture. Puritans like David Clarkson (1621-1686) can help us recover the biblical meaning of this basic doctrine. Educated at Clare Hall, Cambridge, Clarkson was ejected for nonconformity in 1662. Twenty years later, he became colleague and successor to John Owen. His sermon on "The New Creature" is filled with truths that call for many consequences. Clarkson's text comes from Galatians 6:15, where the apostle declares that what really matters is our re-creation.

"The New Creature"

Unless a man be a new creature, no privilege or religious duties will avail him anything as to acceptance with God, or salvation... Baptism, hearing the Word, and prayer, are privileges and duties commanded by God and necessary to be observed... But as to acceptation with God, and salvation, they avail nothing—unless he becomes a new creature.[1]

The unregenerate person lacks faith, and without faith he cannot please God or be saved (Heb. 11:6). If he is not a new creature, he is not in Christ and cannot be saved nor accepted (Acts 4:12). The unregenerate cannot do what is spiritually good, for till the heart be good, nothing that is good can proceed from it (Luke 6:43-49).[2]

The unregenerate builds upon the sand that raises his hopes of heaven upon outward rituals... But, if he is not a new creature, woeful will be the ruin of his hopes in the day of trial.

Whom God calls, he makes them new creatures... Man is made a new creature (2 Cor. 5:17) when the Lord creates new and gracious qualities in his soul. God alone is able for this work (John 3:1-8). Only he can bring about newness of life, creating a new man (Col. 3:10) and restoring the divine image (Eph. 4:24).[3]

So this is called the new birth: a new mind, a new will, and a new person... The old ways of profaneness and ungodliness, the old ways of false worship and of man's invention, the new creature cannot digest. Indeed, when a church is corrupted and God's worship adulterated with man's traditions, a new creature will endeavour to purge out the old leaven... supporting only what is prescribed by God.[4]

Regeneration involves not only the crucifixion of the old man but the resurrection of the new. Leaving behind idolatrous and wicked practices is not sufficient. Temperance, justice, chastity, liberality, prudence, truth, modesty may be found where there is nothing of the new creature. (Decent heathens are still strangers to Christ.) The new creature is the workmanship of the divine power.

Regeneration involves more than an outward conformity to the law of God... His workmanship is within the soul... Nor is a partial change enough. There must be a total change of the whole soul—not only of the understanding, affections, mind, will, conscience, heart, memory... There may be much knowledge of the things of God, clear apprehensions of gospel truth, and assent to revealed doctrine, with persuasions of the truth, and yet no new creature.

What is a new creature? He is a new creature whose soul is made new in all its faculties... renewed according to the image of God, in knowledge, holiness, and righteousness (Col. 3:10; Eph. 4:24).[5] The mind, will, conscience and affections are [made] new in every creature. [He is] renewed by God (Ezek. 36:26)... There are new apprehensions. Once the unregenerate was in darkness. Now his blindness has become light in the Lord. There comes a conviction about the transcendent excellency and absolute necessity of Christ. Once the unregenerate apprehended some pleasure, advantage, safety in sin. But now he sees it as extreme evil, loathsome, dangerous, damnable... That holiness of heart and strictness of life he once slighted, condemned, and derided as a needless or hypocritical preciseness, he now sees as necessary, beautiful, and lovely... He is persuaded of such a necessity of Christ, as he whose neck is on the block is persuaded of the necessity of a pardon to save his life.[6]

Formerly, the unregenerate could have heard and read the promises in the Scriptures without much regarding them... But now he will not part with the riches he sees in gospel promises. Formerly, he had rather have spent his time in merry company than in seeking God or hearing a sermon... but now, one day or even one hour in these holy employments is better in his account than a thousand elsewhere (Ps. 84:10).[7]

Formerly, his church-privileges or religious performances, his alms-deeds, or outward observance of the law... seemed something worthy to make his way to heaven. But now he counts all these but loss, compared with the righteousness of Christ (Phil. 3:7-8).

Formerly, his designs were driven towards sin, himself, or the world. Now they are for God, for heaven, and for his soul.

Formerly, his design was to ingratiate himself with those that might do him good, make him great or safe in the world; now it is to continue in the favour of God, to walk in the light of his countenance and enjoy sweet fellowship with the Father and the Son.

Formerly, his design was to live plentifully and creditably in the world; now it is to get his heart crucified to the world, and the world unto him, to live soberly, righteously, godly in this present world, and walk in it as one redeemed from it...

Formerly, his design was to grow rich, to lay up store for the time to come, to provide plentifully for posterity; now it is to be rich unto God, to partake more and more of the unsearchable riches of Christ, to grow in grace, and abound in the fruits of the Spirit; to lay up treasures in heaven... to bring up posterity in the fear and nurture of the Lord... that they may be heirs of the kingdom that cannot be shaken.

Formerly it was his design to make sure that what he enjoys on earth is secured from... the violence of men; now it is to make his calling and election sure (2 Peter 1:8-11).[8]

The new creature seeks to discover what parts of the Word of God, whether promises or threatenings, or what examples are more suitable to his soul's condition, that he may take special notice of them in hearing and reading... or discover where he lies most open to the assaults of Satan and his spiritual enemies, where sin makes its breaches, so that he may fortify it especially and set a strong guard... Having found out the root of sin, he strikes at that... cutting off corruptions, encouragements, and incentives to sin.[9]

The regenerate person will also study how he may win others to come to Christ, and renounce sin.

Although the dying thief repented at death and was admitted into paradise, we have no reason to defer our repentance and reformation... But what if death is uncertain and the Lord delays his coming? We must be continually watchful and involved in the Lord's work, rather than prove to be unprofitable servants (Matt. 24:48).[10]

In regeneration, the cogitative power of the mind is renewed. Atheistical thoughts... revengeful thoughts, lustful thoughts, proud thoughts, worldly thoughts, anxious thoughts, distempering the mind with fear and distrust... When Christ works this new creation in mind, these are driven out, as were buyers out of the temple. Put away vain, unprofitable, foolish, impertinent, incoherent thoughts. Welcome now into your mind thoughts that are holy, spiritual, heavenly—thoughts of Christ!

The regenerate soul has new objects to counsel about and new counsellors to consult with... It is not the end but the means that he consults about; not whether Christ shall have the highest place in his soul but by what means he may be most advanced... It is the wisdom from above which guides him... He consults with the oracles of God, going for advice to the law and the testimony (Isa. 8:20).[11]

The new creature has a new will, a new heart, directing the regenerate... The most powerful and distinguishing work of renewing grace is in the will... influencing inclinations, intentions, choices, consent, application, and resolutions. The heart, moved by sin, the world, and self, is now carried towards God in Christ—as his chief good, the spring of all his pleasures, the treasury of all his riches.[12]

It is the effect of this great work of God to turn the heart from idols unto God, from the creature to the Creator. Hence it is called conversion... There is an attractive virtue in Christ (John 12:32). This, of course, will be a mystery to those who have had no experience of it.[13]

Set the world, in all its pomp and glory, all its delights and treasure, before the soul on one side, and God as manifested in Christ on the other, and a renewed heart will turn its back on the world and bend itself towards God... A new creature has not a heart for sin and for the world. The fixed, usual, constant bent of his will is towards God as his chief good and only happiness... God is now his end. What he intends above all is to glorify God, please him, and enjoy him.[14]

In choosing a minister, the regenerate will not incline to one who will sew pillows under his elbows, cry peace to him while he lives in sin, or encourage him by doctrine or practice in any evil course; nor to him who will please his fancy with quaintness, notions, or niceties. He will prefer him that will search his conscience, deal faithfully with his soul, not suffer him to live at peace in any wickedness; one who delivers sound, searching, quickening truths and teaches Christ, as the truth in Jesus.[15]

He that will have Christ must deny himself (Matt. 16:24). He must take up the cross, be willing to endure reproaches, afflictions, and persecutions… to lose all if the glory and ways and truths of Christ call for it (Luke 14:26). Whosoever follows Christ must resolve to walk in every way of Christ and to abandon every evil way.[16]

Our resolve to walk in every way of Christ should be permanent and fixed—not forced by some rousing sermon, awakening providence, sharp affliction, or apprehensions of approaching death… When the affliction is removed, or the sermon forgotten, the fear of hell or death vanished, these purposes will vanish too… But when the will is renewed, these resolutions are constant, habitual, durable.[17]

It is not in the power of man to make himself a new creature… It is God's workmanship alone (Eph. 2:10). The means that the Lord has prescribed, however, must be used by those who desire to attain that end. The Lord will concur with the means of his own prescribing… The mariner cannot sail without wind nor can he procure a wind at his pleasure, but he may thrust his vessel off a shore and spread his sails to take advantage of a gale when it blows… Neglect not the means of grace.[18]

But what are these means of grace? Attend the Word preached (James 1:18). This is the incorruptible seed by which you must be begotten (1 Peter 1:23-25). Meditate upon the Word, apply it to your soul, mix it with faith, and act according to it… Consider seriously and frequently the misery of your present unrenewed state… Cry mightily to God for renewing grace.[19]

If the Lord has given you a new heart and a new spirit, be thankful, grateful, and joyful… That which makes us miserable is sin and the effects of sin; but the more you are renewed, the more you will be freed—both from sin and the woeful issues of sin. The more you put on the new man, the more will the old be put off with its affections and lusts. As the cause is removed, the effects will cease… The more renewing grace, the more joy, grace, and glory.[20]

Chapter 7

Radical repentance

David Clarkson, who you were introduced to in the previous chapter, is not a household name, but he deserves to be better known among believers who are serious about the great themes in Puritan preaching. Clarkson's sermon on repentance was typical of Puritan messages that dealt with sin and forgiveness—realities that remain relevant to men and women today.

True repentance

Clarkson took as his text Luke 13:3: "Except ye repent, ye shall all likewise perish" (AV). God's judgements on others should awaken us to repentance while there is time. He calls us to forsake sin (John 5:14), because every sin is pregnant with judgement... Wrath is kindled and burns... Let us learn to tremble, to forsake sin—our own sin. Beware of treating the gospel with contempt—the greatest sin, calling for severest judgement.

It is Christ who admonishes us and summons us to repentance. This is a gospel duty not to be denied. Christ taught repentance, from the start of his ministry (Mark 1:15) to the moment of his ascension (Luke 24:47). The law transgressed leaves no hope for sinners. The gospel, however, calls us to repentance (Acts 17:30-31). This was the message of the apostles, as it had been of the prophets. Recall the preaching of Peter at Pentecost (Acts 2:28) and the letter of John (1 John 1:9). Christ provided them with his personal example, calling sinners to repentance (Matt. 9:13). By his atoning death, and intercession in heaven, he opens the gate for sinners to come back to God.[1]

God gives the remission of sins upon condition of repentance. He does not—he will not—pardon till we repent. Real repentance is the way to life (Acts 11:18). The goodness of God should lead you to repentance (Rom. 2:4). This is part of the gospel of grace and involves nothing meritorious on the part of the penitent. The Lord pardons our sins, loves us, blesses us when we repent, not *because* we repent.[2]

We cannot make amends for sin, since the injury sin has done is infinite, having disobeyed, displeased, and dishonoured an infinite Majesty. We must, therefore, depend on Christ for strength, giving us the ability to repent... He can give us soft hearts that can repent and teach them by his Spirit before they will repent... Except he break those rocks, they will yield no water. Except he breaks these hearts, they will not bleed.[3]

We have no spotless righteousness to present to God but that of Christ. Else we must hide ourselves from the presence of him who sits on the throne. [Christ's] sacrifice is accepted, so that his righteousness becomes imputed to us. His perfection covers our acknowledged defects.

Impenitent sinners are apt to think of themselves not so great sinners as others. Like Pharisees, they try to justify themselves by imagining their innocency and purity. But those that will not repent shall perish.[4]

To repent is to turn from sin (Ezek. 14:6)... and involves a turning to God. In this turning there are three steps: sorrow for sin, hatred of sin, and a resolve to forsake sin. Sorrow for sin means:

1. Affliction of soul, the pain of a contrite heart... a godly sorrow (2 Cor. 7:9-10)... a sense of having sinned against God's authority, mercy, glory, blessedness, holiness, power, truth, sovereignty and excellencies.[5]
2. Hatred for sin—where there is no indignation, no hatred, there is no real repentance.
3. Forsaking of sin; resolving never to sin again: a resolution that is not weak, partial, and relegated to a distant future. The truly penitent must be vigilant against temptation, stand guard, not satisfied with cutting branches, but completely uprooting the tree of evil.[6]

Whom the Lord does not pardon he will punish eternally... no repentance, no pardon... Those who turn not from their sins while they live must die in their sins when they die... A true penitent will aggravate his sins to the utmost; will entertain such thoughts and considerations as may humble him, and increase his sorrow for sin; will be importunate with the Lord to take away the heart of stone; will be often looking on Christ crucified.[7]

Our Lord, in Scripture, determines what is sin: transgression of the law (1 John 3:4). We are commanded to be holy, so the lack of holiness is forbidden... Repentance is a turning from sin; he who does not turn from it does not repent at all.[8]

There is no true repentance where the life is not reformed, but there may be an unblameable life, outwardly reformed, where there is no true repentance... Abstinence from sin, outwardly, is not sufficient... God judges the life by the heart... We must not only cease to do evil, but learn to do good (Isa. 1:16-17). It is not enough to say with the Pharisees, "I am not as other men" (Luke 18:11).[9]

Make haste to repent, that your sins may be blotted out... Our sins made him a Man of Sorrows.

Repentance is the time when all happiness begins, when misery ends... the time from whence you must date all mercies.

The thief on the cross repented when he was dying. But his

repentance at death is no ground to defer repentance till death... All that can be argued from this one example is that it is possible to repent when dying... If you defer repentance till then, it is ten-thousand-to-one you will never repent... There is no reason to draw a rule from an extraordinary instance... It is high presumption, to expect the Lord to save you at your death, if you willfully neglect the ordinary means of salvation all your lives.[10]

The Great Physician

Richard Sibbes was a skilled physician of the soul. For sinners, he did not prescribe penance, but recommended repentance. Sibbes believed that instead of disputing about predestination, we should begin with the wounds of Christ and the love of God. Sibbes also urged "a speedy repentance," a turning away from sin to the true and living God while there was time. Delay could be deadly.[11]

Repentance should cover far more than a general confession. We should confess the particular sin (or sins) to which we are most addicted and guilty. Let there be no dallying with sin.[12]

Sibbes encourages sinners to go to the Great Physician for the healing of the dread disease of backsliding (Hosea 14:2). He will take away:

1. The guilt of sin, which is the venom of it, by justification.
2. The rage of sin, which is the spreading of it, by sanctification.
3. The judgement upon our estate, due to sinners.

When God heals, he heals perfectly, but in some cases slowly. Sanctification takes time.[13]

Because God is a discerner and searcher of the heart, who can see all, and so can cure all, being above the sting of conscience, he has a remedy above the malady.[14]

Christ came from heaven, took our nature upon him, and therein died, satisfying the wrath of God—justly offended with us—by the sacrifice of himself (Isa. 53:10-12). Do we doubt his willingness to

Richard Sibbes

heal us? He comes to us, and calls us (Matt. 11:28). It is his purpose to heal our souls of all our transgressions (Isa. 53:5).[15]

Sin unconfessed, said Sibbes, is like a broken piece of rusty iron in the body. It must be removed, else it will, by rankling and festering, cause more danger. Repentance and remission, however, bring healing. When we confess our sins, he will heal us by the forgiveness of our sins (Ps. 32:4-5).

In the Puritan era, the plain but powerful preaching of God's law prepared the way for the gracious offer of God's gospel. That was the pattern followed by the evangelists of the Reformation, and of every genuine awakening in succeeding centuries. In our time, however, some preachers are reluctant to follow this sequence, out of an unwillingness to be considered politically incorrect or from a fear of being labelled as judgemental. This has fed people a diluted message and lowered their sense of need for grace and repentance.

More than three centuries have passed since the formulation of that basic definition of repentance unto life. It is still valid for us now.

Repentance unto life is a saving grace, whereby a sinner—out of a true sense of his sin, and apprehension of the mercy of God in Christ—does, with grief and hatred of his sin, turn from it unto God with full purpose, and endeavour after new obedience.[16]

Chapter 8

Justified *and* sanctified

In 1677, John Owen produced a treatise on justification by faith through the imputation of the righteousness of Christ. This doctrine, indispensable to the gospel of grace, is fully explained, solidly confirmed, and convincingly vindicated on the basis of Holy Scripture. The purpose of this doctrinal statement is two-fold: the glory of God and the good of all who turn to Christ for peace with God.

The imputation of Christ's righteousness

Owen affirms that justification is the way and means whereby a person, perplexed with a sense of the guilt of sin may obtain acceptance before God, with a right and title to a heavenly inheritance... God pardons all our sins, receives us into his favour, declares and pronounces us righteous and acquitted from all guilt, removes the curse, and turns away all his wrath from us, giving us right and title to a blessed immortality or life eternal. This truth is found in the third and fourth chapter of the letter to the Romans, and elsewhere in Scripture.[1]

It is the direction, satisfaction, and peace of the consciences of men, and not the curiosity of nations or the subtilty of disputations, which is Owen's duty to design by expounding this evangelical doctrine.

Sinners are acquitted or discharged of sin, and accepted with God ... not by their works of righteousness but due to the obedience, righteousness, satisfaction, and merit of the Son of God, our Mediator and Surety of the covenant, imputed to us... This is the only way of relief for those who are in themselves guilty before—or obnoxious and liable to—the judgement of God. Let us not lose the benefit and comfort of this most important evangelical truth in needless and unprofitable contentions... perpetuating endless divisions.[2]

Every true believer, who is taught of God, knows how to put his whole trust in Christ alone... and not at all concern himself with those loads of thorns and briars which, under the name of definitions, distinctions (are merely) exotic, pedagogical, and philosophical terms.[3]

Scripture tells us that God is the one who justifies (Rom. 8:33). He alone blots out our transgressions (Isa. 43:25). It is only in his sight that men are justified or condemned... The whole work of justification... is represented after the manner of a judicial proceeding before God's tribunal—before the greatness, the majesty, the holiness, and sovereign authority of God.[4]

Anselm (1033-1109), in his *Meditations*, expressed these sentiments: "My conscience has deserved damnation, and my repentance is not sufficient for satisfaction, but most certain it is that God's mercy abounds above all offense." Or, as Ambrose (*c*.340-397) put it, "Let no man arrogate anything to himself; let no man glory in his own merits or good deeds; let no man boast of his power; let us all hope to find mercy by our Lord Jesus, for we shall all stand before his judgement-seat. Of him I beg pardon, of him will I desire indulgence. What other hope is there for sinners?"[5]

A clear apprehension and due sense of the greatness of our apostasy from God, of the depravation of our natures thereby, of the power and guilt of sin, of the holiness and severity of the law, are necessary unto a right apprehension of the doctrine of justification... Our recovery and restoration depend only on the satisfaction of Christ and the efficacy of divine grace.[6]

Until men know themselves better, they will care very little to know Christ at all... By the imputation of Adam's transgression, his posterity is corrupted and condemned. But by the imputation of the obedience of Another [i.e. Christ], we may be declared righteous... This is the only way of deliverance and salvation... So we must never be diverted from Christ and seduced to place our confidence in ourselves.[7]

In the gospel there is revealed the way of justification: the imputation of the righteousness of Christ, received by faith (Rom. 1:16-17). Paul excludes from justification everything but the righteousness of God and the faith of believers.[8]

The grace of God, the promise of mercy, the free pardon of sin, the blood of Christ, his obedience, and the righteousness of God in him, rested in and received by faith, are everywhere (in Scripture) asserted as the causes and means of our justification[9]... Renouncing even the best of our obedience and the best of our personal righteousness, we depend wholly on sovereign grace and mercy alone (Ps. 130:3-4). We are justified by faith, without our (imperfect) deeds (Rom. 3:24-28). Blessed is the person to whom the Lord will not impute sin (Rom. 4:2-8). Through the disobedience of Adam all are made sinners, but by the obedience of Another shall many be declared righteous (Rom. 5:12-21). No man is justified by the works of the law in God's sight, but only by faith in Jesus Christ (Gal. 2:16). Salvation is not by any merit on our part. It is a gift received by faith (Eph. 2:8-10). The wisest and safest course for anyone seeking to be justified before God is to betake himself absolutely, his whole trust and confidence, unto sovereign grace and the mediation of Christ—rather than put confidence in merits, pardons, indulgences, and future suffrages for the dead.[10]

The doctrine of justification involves the imputation of our sins to Christ and of his righteousness to us (Lev. 16:21-22). He was made sin for us, who knew no sin, that we might become the righteousness of God in him (2 Cor. 5:21).[11]

Wherefore, by faith thus acting, we are justified and have peace with God. Other foundations in this matter can no man lay that will endure the trial. Yet there are some who obstinately refuse to introduce the mystery of God and his grace into the way of our salvation and our relation to him.[12] They exalt human reason above divine revelation, showing an intolerable presumption... They continually clamour that by our doctrine of the mediation of Christ, we overthrow all obligations to a holy life.[13]

We must not separate justification from the need of holiness or obedience in them that do believe. Justification by the imputation of the righteousness of Christ, and the necessity of our personal obedience... are clearly understood by the exercise of the wisdom of faith. It enables us to comprehend the harmony of the mystery of God, and the consistency of all its parts with one another. The abounding of grace is the principal motive to their abounding in holiness.[14] By the exercise of faith, we are not only justified but we please God.

The doctrine of justification occasioned the Reformation.[15] It was the main hinge on which it turned. In general, no small benefit redounded unto the world by the Reformation... The first Reformers found their own consciences and those of other men so immersed in darkness, so pressed and harassed with fears and terrors... so destitute of any steady guidance into the ways of peace with God that they anxiously sought deliverance... They were either kept in bondage under endless fears and anxieties of mind upon the conviction of sin, or sent for relief to indulgences, priestly pardons, penances, pilgrimages, works satisfactory of their own and supererogatory of others, or kept under chains of darkness for purgatory unto the last day.[16]

We will not come to Christ except as we see that woman whom Christ healed of her issue of blood (Luke 8:43). She had been sick twelve years; she had spent all her substance on physicians, and nobody could help her. This extremity brought her. So we are driven to Christ on our knees, helpless, as low as may be—to show us where help is to be found, and make haste to run to it.[17]

When men have no mind to come to Christ, he sends, as it were, fiery serpents to sting them, that they might look up to the brazen serpent, or rather unto Christ, of whom it was a type, for help (Num. 21:8; John 3:14).

The Reformers laboured diligently in the declaration and vindication of the evangelical doctrine of justification. And God was with them... So they found peace unto their own souls and were instrumental to give liberty and peace with God to the souls and consciences of others, accompanied with the visible effects of holiness of life... unto the praise of God by Jesus Christ.[18]

Justification by faith alone

Justification, as the Puritans and their Reformation predecessors emphasized, was not earned by the merit of our works but received by faith alone. Owen declares that the truth which we plead has two parts. First, that the righteousness of God imputed to us, unto justification of life, is the righteousness of Christ, by whose obedience we are made righteous. Secondly, that it is faith alone which on our part is required to give us a share in that righteousness, or whereby we comply with God's grant and communication of it, or receive it unto our use and benefit. This faith is in itself the radical principle of all obedience.[19]

Many expressions used in the declaration of the nature and work of faith... are metaphorical. They are used by the Holy Ghost, in his infinite wisdom... for the instruction and edification of the church.[20]

That faith whereby we are justified is most frequently in the New Testament expressed by receiving... We are said to receive Christ himself (John 1:12; Col. 2:6). Unbelief is expressed by not receiving him (John 1:11; 12:48)... Faith alone receives Christ, and what it receives is the cause of our justification, whereby we become sons of God. So also we receive the atonement made by the blood of Christ (Rom. 5:11). Thus, too, we receive the forgiveness of sins (Acts 26:18). In receiving Christ, we receive the atonement;

and in the atonement we receive the forgiveness of sins. The grace of God and his righteousness are also received (Rom. 5:17). Since the work of faith in our justification be the receiving of what is freely granted, given, communicated and imputed to us ... then our other graces, our obedience, duties, works, have no influence regarding our justification.[21]

Faith is expressed by looking (Isa. 45:22; Zech. 12:10)... Only they that looked at the brazen serpent were healed of the plague of fiery serpents and lived (Num. 21:8-9; John 12:32). Their healing was a type of the pardon of sin, with everlasting life... Now if faith be a looking to Christ, under a sense of the guilt of sin and our lost condition... then it is exclusive of all other graces and duties whatever. So they who are hopeless, helpless, and lost in themselves ... in a way of expectancy and trust, seek for all help and relief in Christ alone.[22]

Faith is also expressed by coming to Christ (Matt. 11:28; John 6:35,37,45,65). To come to Christ for life and salvation is to believe on him unto the justification of life. But as no other grace or duty is required in coming to Christ, so they have no place in justification... Convinced of sin, weary with the burden of it, anxious to flee from the wrath to come, having heard the voice of Christ in the gospel inviting you to come to Christ for help, your coming to Christ will consist in a complete renunciation of all your own duties and righteousness and turning to Christ alone, and his righteousness, for pardon of sin, acceptance with God, and a right to the heavenly inheritance.[23]

Faith is expressed by fleeing for refuge (Heb. 6:18). It is the flight of the soul to Christ for deliverance from sin and misery... fleeing to Christ as presented in the promise of the gospel, with diligence and speed, that he perish not in his present condition.

Faith is also a leaning on God (Micah 3:11), or on Christ (Acts 11:23); resting on him, cleaving to him, trusting in him, waiting on him. Such believers do everywhere declare themselves to be lost, hopeless, desolate, poor orphans, who place all their hope and expectation on God alone.[24]

Growing more like Christ

The *Westminster Confession* defines sanctification as progressive piety. It begins with the second birth and comes to consummation when God's image is perfectly restored in his people.[25]

The Westminster Divines put it like this:

> They who are effectually called and regenerated, having a new heart and a new spirit created in them, are further sanctified, really and personally, through the virtue of Christ's death and resurrection, by his Word and Spirit dwelling in them; the dominion of the whole body of sin is destroyed, and the several lusts thereof are more and more weakened and mortified, and they more and more quickened and strengthened, in all saving graces, to the practice of true holiness, without which no man shall see the Lord.
>
> This sanctification is throughout in the whole man, yet imperfect in this life: there abideth still some remnants of corruption in every part, whence ariseth a continual and irreconcilable war, the flesh lusting against the Spirit, and the Spirit against the flesh. In which war, although the remaining corruption for a time may prevail, yet through the continual supply of strength from the sanctifying Spirit of Christ, the regenerate part doth overcome; and so the saints grow in grace, perfecting holiness in the fear of God.[26]

The reality of the new birth is evidenced in sincere repentance and saving faith. Puritan preachers plainly but powerfully called sinners to repentance and encouraged their hearers to put their trust in Christ. Such a balanced approach is not always discernable in our time, as the call to faith may be prominent but the summons to repentance for sin is too often muted.

Thomas Watson, who died in 1686, preached a series of sermons (more than 175) on the *Westminster Shorter Catechism*. Published posthumously in 1692, it contains many practical observations designed to further our sanctification.²⁷ Consider his comments on the holiness of God, the most sparkling jewel of his crown… The seraphim acknowledge his holy character and marvel at the reflection of his glory in the universe (Isa. 6:3). God's holiness consists in his perfect love of righteousness and abhorrence of evil (Hab. 1:13). As light is the essence of the sun, so holiness is the essence of God. He is the cause of all that is holiness in others (James 1:17). Since God is so infinitely holy, let us endeavour to imitate God in his holiness (1 Peter 1:16). Our holiness should consist in his image—his meekness, mercifulness, heavenliness; and in submission to his will.²⁸

It is God's great design to make a people like himself in holiness … What is the sending of the Spirit into the world for but to anoint us with the holy unction? And what is the end of Christ's dying but that his blood might wash away our unholiness?

Holiness, says Watson, is the only thing that differentiates us from the reprobate part of the world… Let all that name the name of Christ depart from iniquity (2 Tim. 2:19).²⁹

In 1 Thessalonians 4:3, we are told that God's will is our sanctification. Here are some key points of Watson's sermon on this text.³⁰

Sanctification signifies to consecrate and set to a holy use. It requires mortification, the purging out of sin, which is like defiling leprosy. It also demands vivification, the spiritual refining of the souls, the renewing of the mind… By sanctification, the heart is made holy and is made after God's own heart. A sanctified person bears not only God's name, but his image (Lev. 21:8). Sanctification is a flower of the Spirit's planting… The religion of some consists only of externals, but sanctification is deeply rooted in the soul. And it should be an extensive thing, spreading to the whole person (1 Thess. 5:23). He is holy, whose religion is heated to some degree, and his heart boils over in love to God. Holiness is the quintessence of happiness.³¹

Sanctification is a progressive thing, it is growing, increasing like the morning sun, which grows brighter to the full meridian…

Sanctification is more than mere moral virtue. It is not superstitious devotion... Nor is it hypocrisy, which only makes a pretense of holiness, having a form of godliness but denying its power.[32]

Out of Christ's side came blood and water, blood (symbolic of) justification and water (figure of) sanctification... There is no going to heaven without sanctification (Heb. 12:14). And without it, we can show no sign of our election (2 Thess. 2:13).[33]

To summarize, justification changes our status, while sanctification transforms our character.

William Gouge

Chapter 9

Spiritual *conflict*

In 1627, a Puritan Presbyterian pastor, who was later to be one of the theologians involved in the Westminster Assembly, published a book entitled *The Whole Armour of God*. It was also known as "A Christian's Spiritual Furniture (Equipment) to keep him safe from all the assaults of Satan." This man was William Gouge.

Courage and armour

Based on Ephesians 6:10-18, Gouge's book begins by encouraging believers to be courageous against all sorts of difficulties and dangers that are sure to be encountered by even the best of Christians while they live in this world.[1]

Gouge appeals to all the members of the family of God to be strong with "an inward spiritual strength" in order to face the foe and fulfil Christian duties. As the apostle urged the Corinthians, "Be on your guard; stand firm in the faith; be men of courage; be strong. Do everything in love" (1 Cor. 16:13-14, NIV). Spiritual conflict demands spiritual valour.[2]

The world tries by vain inducements to seduce us (as it drew away Demas). Or else by reproach, trouble, or persecution, to terrify us (as those who forsook Paul). Satan will try to hinder and buffet us. Be brave. Resist the wolf that he may flee.

Remember that our Leader endured the cross and despised its shame. Our foes are many, mighty, and malicious. So be mindful to fight under Christ's banner.[3]

All strength comes from God... We come to be strong by casting ourselves wholly and only upon him and his power. Without Christ, we can do nothing.[4]

We must learn to renounce all confidence in ourselves... our own inability and weakness. Through him, however, we are more than conquerors over our intolerable presumption, filled with spiritual pride that is so derogatory to his glory.[5]

Think of God's omnipotence. Trust in him. Hang your hopes on him... This is a strong prop to our faith, when we trust in the power of God, without wavering or doubting, against fierce lions or cruel dragons and all their hellish host, becoming bold and confident.[6]

The whole armour of God, consisting mainly for safeguard and defense, is made of sanctifying graces... So shall we stand against our foes and resist our enemies. We would count him a madman who would rush naked without any armour into the field among his deadly enemies. Then why face spiritual foes without God's sanctifying graces?[7]

Put on the armour of God—produced and given by him, in keeping with his will. What other armour can stand us in good stead against such enemies? Some foolishly use shields of paper to withstand a musket shot.[8]

Put on the whole armour of God—every grace is to be used... The power of every sanctifying grace must be manifest in the life of a Christian. To imagine that any part of the armour provided by God is unnecessary is to impeach the wisdom of God. If any part is lacking, the devil can take his advantage to destroy the soul.[9]

Single (isolated) graces are counterfeit graces. Faith without righteousness is presumption. Righteousness without truth is hypocrisy... God's assistance and man's endeavours must concur together. Proud papists and careless libertines are both in error... The papists teach that a man may by his free will do well if he will. But libertines go to the other extreme, neglecting the means God has appointed to manifest his power... Many Christians are wounded and foiled by the enemy because of their own idleness and (false) security in that they are backward in arming themselves and negligent in endeavouring to do what God enables them to do.[10]

There is no possibility of remaining safe without spiritual armour. But they who will put on the armour of God and use it as they ought, are safe and sure, and so may be secure. Now whom the devil has in his power, he needs not eagerly pursue. Give all diligence to use the means aright.[11]

Satan, our adversary, is a terrible enemy. He is a fearful tempter, lion, and killer. Remember his power, his malice, his subtlety... He is crafty, using old tricks and new inventions. He can be like a fox, a serpent, or an angel of light, seducing and intimidating. If he cannot seduce by moving men to make light of sin, he will persuade them that every sin is most heinous and unpardonable. He causes schism and breeds heresy. So we need to be strong in the Lord and in the power of his might.[12]

We need to be well armed because we have such an adversary. The greater danger we face, the more watchful and careful we must be for our safety. Watch and pray. Beware of both presumption and despair. Presumption deludes us into supposing that we can handle Satan's temptations, while despair tells us that there is no divine power or pity available to us.[13]

We are involved in a serious and fierce fight... not a light skirmish, but a grappling and hand-to-hand encounter, fierce and dangerous. What the devil did to Christ outwardly and visibly, he does to others inwardly and secretly... No Christian is exempted from this conflict... You should expect to have your heel bruised by the serpent... In a world of wolves, we are like sheep or lambs.[14]

Knowing that the fall of ministers will prove a scandalous discouragement to others, Satan will make the greatest assaults on them. Let ministers know that the precepts they teach others belong to them as well.[15]

Beyond flesh and blood, we have to contend with the devil and his angels. It is no easy matter to prevail against them... The devil has his hand in every temptation... He is the author and finisher of the mischief done by his servants... Therefore, we must strive to drive the devil away, lest he fans in us the fire of lust, pride, greed, and all the other vices.[16]

If we cannot cope with flesh and blood, how shall we overcome principalities and powers? These are evil and malicious spirits over whom the devil reigns. But we are to subject ourselves to the Lord Christ, our King, not as those rebels who would not have him to govern them.[17]

Satan uses fair allurements and fearful terrors to bring the will of man to his bent. He can violently move the air, cause tempests, thunder and lightening... troubling the seas, swallowing up ships... cause earthquakes... stir up pride and greed, and darken man's understanding. Yet Satan's power is limited and restrained by the higher and superior power of God. So we should not take too light a view of Satan, nor dread him too much.[18]

By committing wickedness, we make ourselves the devil's instruments, his imps, and we bear his image. As you carry his image, so surely shall you in hell partake of his punishment and torment—if you repent not.[19]

Be strong and of a valiant courage: fear not, but fight and stand to the end. So shall you be more than conquerors.[20]

The more dreadful and dangerous our enemies be, the more careful ought we to be to stand on our guard and look to our defense. Show defiance, not yielding a hair's breadth to the enemy, who is crafty like a fox and cruel as a lion.[21]

In the time of our greatest tranquility let us meditate on the evil to come... We must through many afflictions enter into the kingdom of God (Acts 14:22). But courage and constancy bring assured conquest and victory.[22]

Our duty is to stand after the battle is ended; with honour and dignity... valiant and courageous, not faint-hearted and weak but as stout, standing soldiers, because we fight in his name, fight a just cause, clad in the armour God provides, and holding fast to his promise of victory.[23]

Stragglers from Christ's armies are separatists, heretics, time-servers, and all rebels. In the commonwealth, in the church, in the family, we have been given a distinct place, and we must be faithful in our particular calling. This requires the avoidance of spiritual slumbering, drowsiness, and worldly cares.[24]

We must persevere... imploring the graces of God's Spirit to our defense (truth, righteousness, patience, faith, and hope) and our offense (God's Word). The Word of God, a sword, is put into our hands so that we may repel and drive away the devil and his instruments... We should never show enemies our backs, never run from them, but stand against them, face to face. If we desert, we put ourselves out of God's protection, and the devil will soon make a prey of us... seeking our destruction.[25]

The Christian soldier is armed from top to toe. His loins are girt about with truth: the truth of judgement (agreeing with God's Word), the truth of heart (sincerity, not hypocrisy), truth of speech (opposed to lying), and truth of action (honest dealing, not deceit)... No eloquence of learning can so grace and commend a man's speech as truth. Lying and falsehood are parts of that foul and filthy communication which the apostle condemns... There is no grace which makes a more notable difference between the children of God and of the devil than truth.[26]

Scripture speaks of Jesus as the truth (John 14:6), of the Spirit of truth (John 16:13), of the Word of truth (John 17:17). God does not lie. Imitate him. See the excellency of truth. Where there is no truth, there can be no trust... The true church is the pillar and ground of the truth (1 Tim. 3:15). So search the Scriptures, frequent the ministry of the Word, find truth. Do not, on any condition, barter it away. Beware of adulterating it... There can be no more sovereign preservative against trouble of conscience than truth of heart.[27]

Truth and righteousness cannot be severed. Righteousness is *conformity to God's law*... a holy quality wrought in us by God's Spirit, whereby we give to everyone his due... This righteousness is a powerful work of God's Spirit in the regenerate, empowering obedience to God's law as we abstain from evil and do what is good—the essential parts of righteousness.[28]

We put on the breastplate of righteousness by the right practice of true repentance—detesting past wickedness and resolving to lead a new life. It keeps us from being mortally wounded, gives us assurance of our eternal election and salvation, while honouring our Lord.[29]

The grace of God has appeared, bringing salvation so that we should live righteously (Titus 2:11-12). We are created and saved to do good works (Eph. 2:8-10). Righteousness testifies of our obedience and thankfulness to God... giving evidence of our election, vocation, and justification.[30]

Next, we consider the shoes of the preparation of the gospel of peace (Eph. 6:15). Do they refer to a readiness to preach the gospel? If so, would it apply only to pastors, evangelists, and missionaries? The gospel of peace is the good news of reconciliation, which pacifies our conscience, prepares our hearts, and works in us that true Christian patience by which we are ready to persevere in our course against all annoyances.[31]

What is the gospel? It is a good message, bringing glad tidings (Isa. 52:7; Rom. 10:15; Luke 2:10-11). This gospel brings peace, our reconciliation with God, bridging the awesome gap caused by man's rebellion against God, dealing with the need to satisfy God's wrath, and offering his favour to man. Christ, the Mediator, is our peace (Isa. 9:6; Eph. 2:14; 2 Cor. 5:19,21).[32]

This gospel of peace enables us to endure and persevere patiently. It would be mere childishness and cowardice to be impatient. Patience is absolutely necessary. Without it, there can be no hope of attaining to victory, glory, and rest where Christ is. If we are thus well shod, no trouble will dismay us or hinder us in our Christian course.[33]

The shield of faith is the next piece of spiritual armour. It alone enables us to quench all the fiery darts of the wicked. Our duty is to take the shield of faith and to quench the devil's fiery darts. Faith is a preeminent grace. No other doctrine more sets forth the glory of God or more benefits the good of his church and his children. In regard to man's good, faith is a most necessary grace. It is profitable and brings comfort. It is a mother-grace, which breeds and brings forth other graces.[34]

By faith, we reach out and touch Christ. By faith, he dwells in our hearts. From faith spring repentance, love, and new obedience... By faith we are reconciled, justified, sanctified, saved... Faith is a grace of admirable comfort, bringing peace of conscience. Therefore, preach about faith. It is the most proper and principal object of the gospel.[35]

Faith is *assent of the mind* to the truth spoken, a belief of God's truth, applicable to the elect (Titus 1:1). Faith is also the *consent of the will* to God's truth. By God's offer of his Son with the gospel, and our receiving of him by faith, we came to be espoused to Christ... The shield of faith protects us against the fiery darts of the devil, such as temptations, doubts, and denials. This faith is a gift of God (Eph. 2:8-9), and comes in connection with the Word that is preached (Rom. 10:14-17). Preaching is God's ordinance by which he gives his blessing. He has committed to preachers the Word of reconciliation, offering the promise of God to all who believe.[36]

God works on the understanding, and then on the will. He exposes man's misery as a sinner, condemned by his breaking of the law with sins of commission and omission. But the preaching of the gospel in the power of the Holy Spirit reveals Jesus Christ, the Son of God, the Saviour who bore away man's sin and God's wrath. So the mind is enlightened, and the will is moved. The gospel heals those who are wounded in conscience... terrified with God's judgements... sorrowing for sin, and desirous of mercy. When they gladly accept the free offer of God, they also receive Christ with all his benefits.[37]

God, in wisdom, has appointed the preaching of his Word as the means of producing faith. And we are encouraged to receive the Word by his free grace and rich mercy. Incredulity is truly and properly a most grievous sin against God and dangerous to men. So we may say, "Lord, I believe; help my unbelief" (John 3:18; Mark 9:24).[38]

True faith is a justifying faith. This is the constant doctrine of our church, taught in our universities, preached in our pulpits, published in print. From faith comes a quiet conscience... From this come two blessed fruits: first, a holy security of mind; second, a spiritual joy of heart... Faith grows through the ministry of God's Word, and the administration of the sacraments. Since God in wisdom has ordained these means to cherish our faith, we ought to be conscientious in a frequent use of them.[39]

By the shield of faith, we may turn aside the temptations of the malicious and mischievous one. We must never forget that these darts are only kept off by faith. The enemy would cause us to disobey and be destroyed. But faith assures us of God's love, so that we rest on his favour revealed in Christ. How wretched must be the condition of those who are destitute of faith! Let us with all speed have recourse to God's promises, and to Christ Jesus, the true Heir of those promises, and so renew our faith... The believer finds no ground of confidence in himself, and therefore, he casts himself wholly on Christ. Such faith rests on a sure ground, which is God's Word.[40]

We are also to take the helmet of hope. It is no easy matter to be a Christian soldier and steadfastly to stand to the end against all assaults. Salvation is the main goal of our hope. We are saved in hope (Rom. 8:24). Hope looks for the fulfillment of all God has promised. We hope in him who neither lies nor disappoints. While faith refers to things past and present, hope relates to what is yet to come... As a helmet covers the head, so hope keeps the head safe from arrows, darts, bullets, swords, and other weapons. It moves forward unafraid, waiting for salvation in the end.[41]

The use of hope is to keep us from fainting, so that we be not confounded through any assaults of our enemies. Hope is the anchor that sees believers through storms and tempests, keeping the ship safe and sure... Hope empowers endurance, and patience, waiting for the fulfillment of God's promises... The purpose of hope is to enable us to wait, and still to wait, and do it patiently... It is the function of hope to make us look so much the more steadfastly upon God, especially since we are prone by nature to suppose that God forgets us and remembers not his promise to us.[42]

Now we come to the sword of the Spirit, which is the Word of God. It is not enough to keep off our enemies' assaults from annoying us. Our care and endeavour must be to drive away those foes and destroy them... This involves mortifying the old nature and crucifying the flesh... According to Romans 13:3-4, magistrates may use the sword of God to cut off and destroy those dangerous and mischievous enemies who plague the nation. This is done by the temporal sword, not by the sword of the Spirit. But God has afforded to magistrates not only the spiritual sword—which is common to all Christians—but also a temporal sword which is proper to them. They must use both against the heretical and profane, and so put Satan to flight.[43]

Ministers must not only teach the truth and instruct the upright, but also restore errors, cut down sin, and endeavour to destroy whatever makes against the glorious gospel of Christ. Let them, therefore, use the two-edged sword by teaching sound doctrine, confuting errors, and reproving sins... Our weapon is the true Word of God, which reveals his will. God is the ultimate Author of Scripture, but ministers must discover the true sense of Scripture in keeping with the fundamental points of our Christian religion. They should compare Scripture with Scripture, obscure places with perspicuous places... the Word of God is of great use, both to defend us from all our spiritual enemies and also to drive away and destroy them. Know, believe, apply, and obey the Word.[44]

There can be no greater enemy to preaching and preachers than ignorance... Ignorance of God's Word is the cause of all error (Matt. 13:19). Ignorance of the Scriptures leads to ignorance of

Christ... a most odious vice, against which Christ will come in flaming fire. To use spiritual armour properly, we must pray in the Spirit with all perseverance... It has pleased God in his unsearchable wisdom to appoint prayer as a means to obtain all needful blessings at his hands.[45]

The importance of prayer

William Gurnall (1617-1679) was pastor of the Church of Christ in Lavenham, Suffolk, for thirty-five years and committed to the Reformed faith. He is mainly known for his classic on spiritual warfare, *The Christian in Complete Armour*. Like the treatise produced by William Gouge, it expounds and applies Ephesians 6:10-18 in considerable detail. And, along with Gouge, Gurnall concludes with an emphasis on prayer. We are to pray with all perseverance—fulfilling the duty of prayer with "invincible patience, courage, and constancy... in prosperity, as well as in adversity."[46]

We are no longer engaged in a campaign to conquer Canaan under leaders such as Joshua or Gideon. Today we do not face Amorites, or Ammonites, Hittites, Hivites, Moabites, or Midianites. Girgashites, Jebusties, and Perizzites pose no obstacle to our advance. But we do encounter enemies ever deadlier. Victory will not come by man's might or the people's power but only by the Spirit of the Almighty (Zech. 4:6). The apostle Paul, a veteran of spiritual conflict, puts us on alert. He says: "Though we live in the world, we do not wage war as the world does. The weapons we fight with are not the weapons of the world. On the contrary, they have divine power to demolish strongholds. We demolish arguments and every pretension that sets itself up against the knowledge of God, and we take captive every thought to make it obedient to Christ" (2 Cor. 10:3-5, NIV). "Thanks be to God! He gives us the victory through our Lord Jesus Christ" (1 Cor. 15:57).

Chapter 10

🌿🌿🌿🌿🌿🌿🌿🌿

Bread and wine

William Tyndale (c.1494-1536) was a precursor of the Puritan movement. He believed in the absolute necessity of the Bible to be translated into English for the development of competent preachers and the enlightenment of believers.[1] The church hierarchy, however, was opposed to his translation project, and he was forced into exile in Europe, hounded by spies and agents. Despite the opposition, Tyndale was able to complete his English translation of the New Testament in 1525.

Commenting on the Lord's Supper, Tyndale noted that *faith alone* satisfies the hunger and thirst of the soul. He taught that the elements of this sacrament remained bread and wine, but signified or symbolized the body and blood of our crucified Saviour. For his views on the Word and the sacrament—betrayed by someone posing as a friend—Tyndale was imprisoned, strangled, and burned at the stake near Brussels on October 6, 1536.

The controversy over the Lord's Supper, however, continued. Peter Martyr Vermigli, a refugee from the Roman Inquisition who was granted a professorial post at Oxford through the Archbishop of Canterbury, Thomas Cranmer (1489-1556), was involved in a crucial debate with several representatives of the traditional view known as transubstantiation. Its advocates believed that the elements *actually* changed into the body and blood of Christ, so that every time the mass was celebrated the Lord Jesus would be sacrificed again. What Rome's representatives understood in a literal sense, Vermigli interpreted figuratively. He emphasized the role of faith, which enabled believers to perceive the meaning of the bread and wine as symbols of Christ's once-for-all sacrifice for our sins. Vermigli insisted that the change was not in the elements but in the participants who, by faith, feed on the saving virtue of the crucified Christ. The resurrection body of our Lord is now ascended into heaven, from whence he shall come to judge the living and the dead.[2]

Preparation and purpose

Henry Smith (1550-1591) was known as a silver-tongued preacher whose popularity was amazing. His ministry at a fashionable London congregation featured the need of validating a profession of faith by the practical pursuit of holiness. Smith produced a treatise on the Lord's Supper in two sermons.[3] The first was based on 1 Corinthians 11:23-24. Smith thought of Scripture and the sacraments as the two breasts wherewith our mother (the church) nurses us. He said that the Lord's Supper is a witness of God's promises, a reminder of Christ's death, and a seal of our adoption. Smith emphasized the need of preparing well to participate in the Eucharist. He noted these points:

1. To Christ belongs the power to ordain sacraments in his church… as bread and wine nourish us in our present life, so the wounded body and shed blood of Christ nourish us in life eternal.
2. Christ instituted this sacrament on the night of his betrayal, a dark night, threatening to eclipse the sun.
3. He took the bread and the cup, giving thanks for what had to be broken and outpoured. To feed on Christ is nothing

but coming to him and believing in him. The bread of eternal life is not eaten with teeth... but spiritually, with faith... All the blessings of Christ are apprehended by faith... Mary was not blessed because Christ was in her body, but because Christ was in her heart.[4]

4. The purpose of this sacrament is to remember Christ crucified for us... the wounding of his body, the shedding of his blood, for our salvation... This sacrament is but a sign of his sacrifice.

Smith's second sermon on the sacrament was based on 1 Corinthians 11:25-28. God's law was given to condemn and mortify our old nature. The gospel, however, is to confirm our new covenant with God and to comfort us. The purpose of Christ was to tie our faith wholly to himself, that we should not seek for anything apart from him.[5]

Stretch forth your hand, and here is Christ's hand, which takes God's hand and man's hand, and joins them together, and then the remission of sins is sealed. The greatest benefit in all the world is to be pardoned and set at liberty.[6]

The gospel has nothing to do with popish merits of works or penances.[7]

We have three invincible arguments against transubstantiation in one verse: we eat bread, not flesh; we are to represent (not repent) his death; we are to remember him till he come.[8]

Self-examination is required before receiving the elements. We are to examine ourselves as to our faith, love, and repentance, before coming to this feast.

God examines with trials, the devil with temptations.[9]

Become your accuser and judge... make your heart the foreman of the jury... beware, for every man is partial to himself, even when he is most humbled.[10]

Examine yourself as to your faith, for every heresy is contrary to some article of our belief as every sin is against some of the Ten Commandments.

Do you have faith, not only to believe that Christ died but that he died for *you*, and that he is *your* Redeemer? Are you in charity, loving even your enemies? Do you repent, not only for your open and gross sins but also for your secret and petty sins? Do you resolve never to sin again for any cause... and to begin now and last unto death?

Can you find it in your heart to die for Christ, as Christ died for you... follow him and bear his cross... as servants who obey and soldiers ready to suffer?[11] If you cannot, Smith concludes, remember the text that is: Examine yourselves before you receive this sacrament.[12]

The blessing of the Lord's Supper

John Owen has also left us with several observations on these Eucharistic passages of Scripture. On December 10, 1669, he preached on 1 Corinthians 10:16 and emphasized the truth that Christ was engaged in a great and glorious cause: to deliver all God's elect from death, hell, Satan, and sin.[13] He atoned for all the sins of all the elect, enduring the penal desertion of God.[14] We cannot imagine the unspeakable extremity of the things he suffered. Again, on December 24, 1669, Owen preached on 1 Corinthians 11:26. He declared that the great work of the ministry is to represent Jesus Christ—by preaching the Word and administering the sacrament.[15] His sermon on 1 Corinthians 11:28, preached in January 1670, stressed the "needful duty" of self-examination. Aware of the presence of God (Isa. 57:15), we are to cleanse our hearts and hands, confronted with an immediate sense of the authority and command of God.[16]

John Flavel, a son of the manse, whose ministry involved both preaching and writing, authored a volume entitled *The Fountain of Life*. Flavel died in 1691, but what he wrote is still helpful today.

Jesus, said Flavel, prepared for his death by praying to the Father and instituting the Lord's Supper. This is recalled by the apostle Paul in 1 Corinthians 11:23-34. Our Saviour has given us the memorial of his death, to be observed in all the churches, until his second coming.[17] Four things are underlined by the apostle: first, the author of the sacrament is Christ, moved by his royal power and authority; second, the timing, after the Passover and before his betrayal; third, it consists of memorative, significative, and instructive signs of bread and wine, and the glorious mysteries represented by them: Christ crucified; four, because we are tempted to forget, we are exhorted to faithful observance.[18]

The memorial Christ left us, wrote Flavel, is a special mark of his love and care... his scars and wounds are emblems of love and honour. Here we have a gracious remembrance of Christ and such a remembrance of Christ includes faith, discerning the Crucified with the precious eye of faith.[19] So we contemplate the wisdom that contrived the glorious and mysterious design of redemption. We also see a representation of the severity of God and his indignation against sin—the revelation of his wrath.[20] Such remembrance produces a humble adoration of the goodness and mercy of God, in exacting satisfaction for our sins by such bloody stripes. Christ bore the wrath of God for our sins.[21]

By this rite, Christ has made abundant provision for the enlargement of the joy and comfort of his people. So we approach the Lord's Table with reverence and rejoicing as he makes himself known to us in the breaking of bread (Luke 24:30-34).[22] This rite also helps us mortify sin, for on that table our corruptions are sacrificed and slain by the Lord.[23] By this ordinance, believers are more strongly bound—the many partake of the same elements. We are at one in the struggle against sin and one in our appreciation of Christ's redemptive work.

Are you easily overcome by temptations? This is the most powerful restraint: to be crucified with Christ. Are you afraid your sins are not pardoned? See the cup of the new covenant, representing the blood of Christ shed for the remission of sins. Then who shall lay anything to the charge of God's elect?

Do you idle away precious time and waste your life in trivial pursuits? Remember that you are not your own. Your time and talents belong to him who bought you with the price of his precious blood

(1 Cor. 6:19-20).[24] The beauty of the Rose of Sharon is never lost or withered. He is the same, yesterday, today, and forever… Blessed be God for Jesus Christ.[25]

Chapter 11

Renewal *and* reform

How can a church, "by schisms rent asunder and heresies distressed," experience renewal and reform? Will it recover from decline through the formation of evangelical fellowships that are like little islands in a sea of denominational liberalism? Will the situation improve by implementing the sort of ecumenism that produces amorphous conglomerates whose agenda is shaped by the world rather than the Word? Is relevance recoverable by the dilution of sound doctrine; or, by prescribing superficial choruses repeated repeatedly (or by proscribing any praise selection composed after the days of Moody and Sankey)?

The Puritans, faced with such possibilities, would surely say "no" to all the above. They were persuaded that renewal and reform could be achieved only when the church is committed to the glory of Christ, listening to what his Spirit says in the Scripture and responding with a willing and grateful obedience.

The true church of Christ

The elect, united with Christ and committed to obedience, are his church (Acts 20:28; Eph. 5:32). The church of Christ, according to John Owen, is the whole company of God's elect, called by God by his Word and Spirit, out of their natural condition to the dignity of his children. United to Christ, who is their Head, they fulfil his great commission: to make disciples of all nations (Matt. 28:18-20; Acts 2:42-47; Heb. 12:22-24; Eph. 2:11-13; Col. 1:15-20). The whole church, however, is not always in the same state. A part of it may be militant, and the other triumphant. The militant church serves and struggles in the present against the world, the flesh and the devil (Eph. 6:10-18; Heb. 11:13-14; 12:1-4). The church triumphant has fought the good fight, kept the faith, and now rests from its labours in heaven (Eph. 5:27; Rev. 3:21; 14:13). Owen sees believing Jews of the Old Testament and Gentiles who come to faith in Christ as being essentially one people of God (Eph. 2:11-16; 1 Cor. 10:31-33; Gal. 4:26-27; Heb. 11:16,26,40). He is convinced that the true church cannot be wholly overthrown on earth, although it may experience seasons of decline and decay as well as recovery and growth. But the gates of hell shall not prevail against it (Matt. 16:18; 1 Tim. 3:15-16; 2 Tim. 2:19).

Owen describes the way and means of recovery from spiritual decadence and obtaining fresh springs of grace. It has mainly to do with *the steady focus of faith on the glory of Jesus Christ*. Breaches are repaired and backslidings healed, when we concentrate on him. He alone can support us under the troubles and temptations of life (2 Cor. 4:16). This is true not only for the individual believer but also for the church.[1]

The glory of kings is in the wealth and peace of their subjects; and the glory of Christ is in the grace and holiness of his subjects... And we derive our spiritual life and grace from him... When this abounds in us so as to give us strength and vigour in the exercise of grace, we will be kept from decays and withering and be strong and healthy... We will be fruitful in all duties of holy obedience. Let us never forget that the way we are made partakers of this grace is by a steady view of the glory of Christ, as is proposed to us in the gospel... Peace in a spiritually decaying condition is soul-ruining security; better be under terror on the account of surprisal in some sin than be in peace under evident decays of spiritual life.²

Spiritual decay

Notwithstanding these blessed promises of growth, flourishing, and fruitfulness, if we are negligent in the due improvement of the grace we have received and the discharge of the duties required of us, we may fall into decay and be kept in a low, unthrifty state all our days. And this is the principal ground of the discrepancy between the glory and beauty of the church as represented in the promises of the gospel and that which is exemplified in the lives of some who merely profess but do not live up to the condition of their accomplishment in them... But the grace promised to this end will not come to us while we are asleep in spiritual sloth and security.³

Fervent prayer, using well the grace received, obedience in holy duties—all these are signs of spiritual life dependent on the Word of God and all other ordinances of divine worship. Yet believers are subject to decays: a gradual decay, in the loss of our first faith, love, and works; in the weakening of the internal principle of spiritual life, with the loss of delight, joy, consolation; and the abatement of the fruits of obedience. Our Lord Jesus Christ expressly charges such decline on five of the seven churches of Asia (Rev. 2-3). And in some of them, as with Sardis and Laodicea, those decays had proceeded to such a degree that they were in danger of utter rejection.

To be overtaken with the effects of sloth, negligence, or the want of a continual watch in the life of faith leads down to the chambers of death. I wish it were otherwise... The glory of Christ, the honour of the gospel, and the danger of the souls of men call for diligence.⁴

The secret root of all our evil will not be removed unless it be digged up. Who sees not, who complains not of the loss of, or decays in, the power of religion in the days wherein we live? But few there are who either know or apply themselves, or direct others, to the proper remedy of this evil... It is almost as difficult to convince men of their spiritual decays as it is to recover them from them. But without this, healing is impossible. If men know not their sickness, they will not seek for a cure.[5]

The church of Laodicea was sensibly delayed, and gone off from its primitive faith and obedience. Yet she was so sure in her condition, knew so little of it, that she judged herself—on the contrary—to be in a thriving, flourishing state. She thought herself increased in gifts and grace, while she was "wretched, and miserable, and poor, and blind, and naked" (Rev. 3:17). ... So it is with many churches in this day, especially that which boasts itself to be without error or blame... It has nothing but a noise of words.[6]

If men will not learn and confess their spiritual decays, there is no hope of prevailing with them to return to the Lord... Such persons are under the power of a stupid security... So we have as little success for the most part in calling persons to look for revival and recovery... A decaying spiritual state and solid spiritual peace are inconsistent.

Pride, selfishness, worldliness, levity of attire, and vanity of life, with corrupt communication, abound among so many... All flesh has corrupted its way... Sloth, indifference, and negligence in the observation of the duties of divine worship, both in private and public, is notorious... Men may draw near to God with their lips, but their hearts are far from him... We hear the Word preached, but do we do it with the same desire... as before?[7]

Grown full of themselves and of a good conceit of their own abilities, men have lost their spiritual appetite for the Word of God. This makes the Word lose its power and efficacy, so that it has little or no taste for them. If they were hungry, they would find a sweetness in the bitterest of its reproofs, beyond what they can now find in the sweetness of its promises... This loss of a spiritual appetite is an evidence of decay in all other graces... They are unwilling to comply with the calls of God to repentance and reformation.[8]

How may believers be delivered from these decays? How may

they come to thrive and flourish within and produce the fruits of spiritual life?[9]

No duties of mortification [of sin] should be prescribed to this end if their matter and manner not be of divine institution and command... Some, like the Pharisees, have invented and enjoined a number of works, ways, duties, which God never appointed or approved, nor will accept.

Convinced of spiritual decays, oppressed with a sense of the guilt of sin, we must see that sin has brought us into that condition.[10]

Means of spiritual restoration

When God designs to heal the backsliding of his people by sovereign grace, he gives them effectual calls unto repentance, and the use of means for their healing... There is no other way to prevent their ruin but by returning to the Lord.[11]

Our backslidings should be healed in a way suited to the glory of God: in fervent prayer, seeking the pardon of all iniquity and requesting God to receive us graciously; confession of the sin wherein backsliding consists; renewal of a covenant engagement to renounce all other hopes and expectations and trust completely in his grace and mercy... This is the method of God's dealing with the church. Then, and then only, we may expect a gracious reviving from all our decays, when serious repentance is found in us.[12]

All our supplies of grace are from Jesus Christ... without him, we can do nothing (John 15:3-5). He is our life efficiently, and lives in us effectively (Gal. 2:20; Col. 3:1-4).

The only way of receiving supplies of spiritual strength and grace from Jesus Christ, on our part, is faith. By faith we come to him, abide with him, live by faith in him, receive grace from him. This faith respects the person of Christ, his grace, his whole mediation, with all the effects of it, and his glory in them all... A constant, lively exercise of faith relying on him, as he is revealed to us in the Scripture, is the only effectual way to obtain a revival from under our spiritual decays and such supplies of grace as shall make us flourishing and fruitful (Isa. 45:22).[13]

A look unto Christ as crucified... is the cause and foundation of that godly sorrow which is a spring of other graces... It is also the way of desiring strength from him, enabling us to endure all our trials, troubles, afflictions, with patience, to the end (Heb. 12:2). This exercise of faith is accompanied by a transforming power and efficacy, changing us every day more and more into the likeness of Christ... Let us live in the constant contemplation of the glory of Christ, and virtue will proceed from him to repair all our decays, to renew a right spirit within us, and to cause us to abound in all duties of obedience.[14]

Chapter 12

Family values

Ulysses and his crew were faced with deadly danger as they made their way between Scylla and Charybdis, off the rugged Sicilian coast. On one side, a whirlpool with its mortal vortex; on the other, jagged rocks and fatal reefs. So it is with Christian behaviour. We must thread our way through legalism and antinomianism. Antinomianism sees law as a tyrannical interference with the life of the individual. Love, not law, is to shape decision in a given situation. To be saved by grace is misinterpreted as being free from moral imperatives. There may be situations in which murder or adultery are not only permissible but advisable. Legalism, on the other hand, imagines that you can legislate *ad infinitum* to cover every situation. We are told that by following a man-made list of "do's and don'ts" we can earn, merit, and eventually, attain salvation.

The truth is that we cannot obey God's commandments to perfection and must rely only on the sacrifice of Christ to pay the debt we owe and the penalty we deserve (Gal. 3:10,24). It is also true that the law was given that we might seek grace, and grace was granted that we might fulfil law. The Ten Commandments are the revelation of God's will, showing us our responsibility to him and to one another.

Our Lord puts the matter clearly when he says: "If you love me, keep my commandments... he who has my commandments, and keeps them, loves me" (John 14:15,21). Here are some comments on these texts from the exposition of this gospel by George Hutcheson (1615-1674), minister at Edinburgh, in 1657:

> The disciples should love Christ and evidence the same by observing his commandments... Affection should flow in the channel of diligence about duty... Obedience to his commandments is the true touchstone and evidence of love to Christ... He puts them in mind of duty and affirms his right as a law-giver to give commandments to his people... He knows their burden and is ready to enable them to obedience... A variety of duties are imposed upon believers, as it is the will of Christ that none of them be slighted... To be obedient, they must have a high estimation of the authority of the law and the excellency of the thing commanded... Many profess love to Christ who yet neglect their duty... The love of God in Christ preceeds our love and obedience to him.[1]

There are at least three of the Ten Commandments that bear on the matter of family values: "Honour your father and your mother... You shall not commit adultery... You shall not covet your neighbour's house... your neighbour's wife... or anything that belongs to your neighbour" (Exod. 20:12,14,17). What the Lord God said through Moses is applied and amplified by his servant Paul. Writing to the Ephesians, he reminded them that husbands and wives should submit to one another out of reverence for Christ; that wives should submit to their husbands as the church should do to her divine head; that husbands should love their wives as Christ loved the church and sacrificed himself for her; that husband and wife become one flesh (Eph. 5:21-33). Children have the obligation to obey their parents because it is the right thing to do, and fathers should avoid exasperating their children. Instead, they ought to bring them up in the training and instruction of the Lord (Eph. 6:1-4). With this as context, we come to consider the comments of several Puritan divines on a parallel passage, Colossians 3:18-21.

Already, in the Colossian letter, the apostle has reminded his readers that Christians are being restored in keeping with the Creator's image. As God's chosen people, they are to give evidence of their election by clothing themselves with compassion, kindness, humility, gentleness, and patience. Forbearance and forgiveness should also characterize them, and love ought to bind them together in genuine unity. The peace of Christ should rule in their hearts, true wisdom be seen in their dealings with one another, and worship offered up with grateful hearts (Col. 3:10-17). All these qualities are to be manifested in family relationships.

Marriage

Henry Smith, the popular Puritan preacher at fashionable St. Clement Danes in London, presented a "Preparative to Marriage." He viewed marriage as a relationship contracted in the Lord, of two to be made one, preceded by longing and affection. Marriage, Smith asserted, is nothing but a communion of life between man and woman joined according to the ordinance of God.[2] Before man had any other calling, he was called to be a husband. Marriage was ordained in paradise, the happiest place... It is the honour of woman to bear children in marriage.[3]

If Christ be at your marriage, if you marry in Christ, your water shall be turned into wine.[4]

Husbands and wives are like oars to a boat. Their marriage cannot stand if they are divided... Husbands, remember that her cheeks were made for your lips, and not for your fists... He is a shameless man who lays hands on his wife. He should be sent to Bedlam till his madness be gone.[5]

A wife is called a yoke-fellow, to show that she should help her husband in his labours, troubles, sickness... with her strength and counsel.[6] A good wife keeps her house. Remember that when

Adam was away, Eve was made a prey.[7]

To her silence and patience she must add that acceptable obedience which makes a woman rule while she is ruled.[8] Frizzled locks, naked breasts, (cosmetic) painting, perfume, and especially a roving eye, are forerunners of adultery.[9]

A husband should represent Christ in his house—teach like a prophet, pray like a priest, and rule like a king.

Marriage is for the propagation of children, the avoidance of fornication, and of loneliness—the inconvenience of solitariness. Else life would be miserable and irksome.[10]

We are taught to marry in the Lord. Then we must also choose in the Lord. Smith concludes: "Thus have I outlined the way to prepare you for marriage. May the Lord, in whom you are contracted, knit your hearts together, that you may love one another and so begin, proceed, and end in his glory."[11]

Family life

In 1614, another London preacher, Edward Elton (*d*.1624), expounded Colossians 3:18-21. Elton's work was published again in 1620, and it is still a useful guide for the development of family life. Elton comments:

> For wives to show obedience and submission is a matter of decorum, comeliness, and decency. But it should only and always be in the Lord, agreeable to the will of God. The motivation is to please God, and so withstand the common enemy... If the husband be a man frantic or mad, one altogether bereft of the use of reason, then surely the wife is not bound to subject herself to his government... A wife's obedience is limited to what is in the Lord, neither contrary to nor different from the Word of God. A rebellious woman is an uncomely and loathsome creature in the sight of God, though her face be never so fair, her beauty is but a ring of gold in a swine's snout... Let Christian wives think on these things.[12]

Elton observes that men ought not to be unkind, bitter, and insensitive to their wives. Their duty is to express affection in word and deed. The apostle does not say: husbands, rule over your wives and exercise authority over them, but he reminds them to *love* their wives.[13] The practice of rule and government must be seasoned with love and sweetness. It is difficult for a man to avoid a domineering and tyrannical attitude, especially if he is not open to the sanctifying grace of God's Spirit. Husbands should use their authority in a holy manner, labouring to have their hearts sanctified, avoiding all rigour and bitterness.[14]

The love of the husband to his wife must be as the love of Christ to his church, protecting, providing, and preserving her. Follow his example... dread adultery, which is the bane of wedlock... Even though the husband be a king, or the greatest man on earth, if he be a husband he must carry in his heart a chaste affection for his wife... loving her, body and soul, contenting himself with her love alone... loving her as he loves himself.[15] He must not be as those who spend in vain and unthrifty company, in the ale-house or like place, and let wife and children starve at home. Such a man runs the risk of becoming a monster among men... fitter to live in Bedlam than in a civil society, driven by the violent passion of anger.[16]

Children are to share a willing and hearty obedience, sound and sincere, accepting admonition, reproof, or correction. Such obedience, however, is not unlimited. It refers only to all things honest and lawful, agreeable to the Word of God. (This sort of obedience not only shows respect for parental authority but expresses gratitude for their paternal care.) Such obedience, pleasing to the Lord, will come from a sanctified heart, from the root of a sound justifying faith, with regard to God's glory.[17]

Fathers ought not to provoke their children, exasperating them by disgraceful and unreasonable demands... treating them with undue severity... Be neither too rigorous nor too indulgent. Correct your child with compassion in your heart.[18]

In 1615, another exposition of Colossians was produced by

Nicholas Byfield (1579-1622), the vicar of Isleworth, London. Commenting on Colossians 3:18 and following, he noted that God's Word sets the standard for family values. Byfield stressed that if it was the wife's duty to be submissive, it was also the man's obligation to love his wife as he loved himself. He preached this at a time when some supposed that ministers should not meddle by telling them how to live at home.[19]

Like other Puritan preachers, Byfield was no prude in dealing with the matter of human sexuality. He emphasized the need of chastity and fidelity. He also denounced the immorality that consumes men's strength, wastes men's substance, surrounds men with evil, is hateful in God's sight, disgraceful to others, and destructive to body and soul.[20]

Nurturing children

Citing the example of Jesus, who was obedient to Joseph and Mary as he grew up in Nazareth, Byfield encouraged children to obey their parents. Likewise, parents were under sacred obligation to nurture their children and avoid the harshness that would break their spirit. Rather, they should pray for them, that God may guide their hearts for their well-being. To do otherwise is to cause anger and discouragement, opening the door to the devil, who sows hellish seeds in their hearts and stirs up impious thoughts. It is not enough to learn that we should abstain from sin. We must also abstain from all provocations to sin, as parents who are accountable to God for their children.[21]

The Westminster Divine, William Gouge, was not only concerned for church and nation: he wanted to see families develop along biblical lines, indispensable to the well-being of society. In his book *Domestical Duties*, published in 1622, he expresses this conviction:

> Piety is the best thing that a parent can teach a child, for as reason makes a man different from a beast, and as learning and civility make a wise and sober man differ from savages and

swaggerers, so piety makes a sound Christian much more to differ from the most civil and well-ordered natural man that can be... Learning, civility, calling, portion, are all nothing without piety.[22]

Chapter 13

☙☙☙☙☙☙☙☙☙

Most *blessed* assurance

Charles Hodge (1797-1878) was an influential exegete and theologian who taught at Princeton at a time when his Reformed convictions were being challenged by liberal revisionists and evolutionary theories. Commenting on the eighth chapter of Paul's letter to the Romans, Hodge noted a rock-solid basis for Christian assurance:

1. We are set free from the condemnation of the Law by the sacrifice of Christ (Rom. 8:1-4);
2. Our salvation has begun with the regeneration and sanctification wrought by the Spirit (Rom. 8:5-11);
3. Since we are children of God, we are also heirs with Christ (Rom. 8:12-17);
4. Our affections are insignificant in comparison with the glory yet to be revealed (Rom. 8:18-28);
5. We are predestined to the attainment of eternal life (Rom. 8:29-30);
6. Because God has given his Son to die for us, our justification and salvation are assured (Rom. 8:31-34);

7. God's love is infinite and immutable, and nothing can separate us from it (Rom. 8:35-39).

This doctrine was the theme of much Reformed preaching during the Puritan era. The pastor of St. Helen's, London, preached without notes but not without preparation. And what he preached in public, he practiced in private. Thomas Horton (d.1673) aimed at the reformation of a society that had become so corrupt that some contemporaries described it as a spurious generation morbid in body and slavish in soul, devoted to spiritual and carnal fornication. Horton studied at Emmanuel College, Cambridge. Master of Queen's College, Vice-Chancellor of Cambridge University and Professor of Divinity at Gresham College, he was dedicated to preaching God's Word in the power of God's Spirit. Posthumously, in 1674, his series of forty-six sermons on Romans 8 was published. Two centuries later, Charles Haddon Spurgeon (1834-1892) expressed his appreciation of Horton's works in these words: "A marvelous homiletical exposition. Horton's discourses are very full of divisions, but then he always has plenty of solid material to divide. Ministers will find teeming suggestions here."

These quotations are drawn from the 645 pages of Horton's exposition, providing believers with a most blessed assurance.

Horton on Romans 8

It is the great advantage and privilege of the saints and servants of God, that whatever befalls them, God is sure to take care of their salvation, and to provide for their blessed state and condition in another world.[1]

God's children are in Christ Jesus. This is the state and condition of all those who are regenerate and true believers… The union of believers with Christ is described in Scripture in a variety of ways: first, that between husband and wife; second, the union of the members with the Lord, a union of incorporation; thirdly, of branches with the Vine, bringing forth much fruit as they partake of his virtue; lastly, of the stones in a building, with the foundation that is Christ.[2]

What are the causes and grounds of this union? First, we are knit to Christ and made one with him by his Spirit... quickened and enlivened by that Spirit. If anyone has not the Spirit of Christ, he is none of his. Secondly, we are knit to Christ by faith, a special gift and fruit of the Spirit.[3]

There is a three-fold mysterious union in Scripture. The first is the union of three persons in one nature; the second is the union of two natures in one person; and third, the union of natures and persons together in one quality or condition. In the first we have one God; in the second, one Mediator; in the third, we have one church... Being one with him, we should behave ourselves suitably to him... Union with Christ and holiness of life are inseparable. Negatively, God's people walk not after the flesh... By "flesh" we are to understand corrupt nature, unsanctified and unregenerate, (infecting) feelings, mind and will. Positively, they walk after the Spirit, in newness of life, as a colony of heaven on earth. They are guided by the Spirit... living according to the line and square of God's holy Word.[4]

The head does not go one way, and the body's members go in another. They must both go in the same direction... The union of a believer with Christ is not empty or fruitless, but powerful and efficacious (John 15:5). It is not enough to abstain from acts of wickedness. We must also perform acts of goodness... Persons united to Christ have freedom and exemption from wrath and condemnation... Because of what Christ has done for them and of what he is to them, it is impossible that they should ever be damned.[5]

Jesus Christ is the Lamb of God who takes away the sin of the world (John 1:29). Christ has satisfied the justice of the Father for all his elect by dying for them (Gal. 3:13). He has taken away the guilt of sins, freed us from condemnation and imputed his righteousness to us... Being justified, we cannot be condemned. He has fully paid the debts which were owing on our account. If the Head lives, the members (of his body) shall live also.[6]

No condemnation in Christ, nothing but condemnation out of Christ.[7]

Romans 8:2 declares that the Spirit of life makes us free from the law of sin and death... There is a two-fold benefit which all believers receive from Christ: the benefit of justification in the acquitting and absolving of their persons, and that of sanctification, in the killing and subduing of their corruptions. Both are exhibited to us in this verse.[8]

Sin in the unregenerate exercises a tyrannical power over them. Consider the sin of immorality which so much abounds at this present time in the world, and how pitifully it captivates people... The dominion of sin is the greatest slavery in the world.[9]

Our nature, once debased by sin, is now exalted by grace... Now, in Christ, our nature is pure and undefiled in God's sight... We are accepted of him as if we had been born without any corruption... There is no condemnation to them that are in Christ Jesus. Why? Because the righteousness of Christ is imputed to them, and reckoned as theirs... Secondly, it holds good in point of sanctification: the pure and holy nature of Christ is the spring and origin of all holiness in us.[10]

In Romans 8:3, we see that the law could not justify us, or free us from sin and condemnation... The law does not offer us any pardon of those things which are done against the law. It has an accusing, but not absolving power... This is rather the work and business of the gospel (Acts 13:38-39). The law shows us our duty, but does not enable us to do our duty. The law could not justify us, or free us from sin and condemnation... Paul points out the defect of the moral law in this business of the justification of a sinner... The law does not offer us any pardon or forgiveness, but it has an accusing power—but not an absolving power... the gospel, however, is the ministration of glory, bringing life with it.[11]

There is a two-fold power or tyranny which is considerable in the nature of sin: the commanding power and its condemning power... It carries the sinner to the transgression of God's law, and then binds the sinner over to punishment for that transgression... But there is a two-fold benefit which all believers receive from Christ: the benefit of justification (acquitting and absolving of their persons) and the benefit of sanctification, killing and subduing their corruptions. If we are in Christ Jesus, and his Spirit of life is in us, we will be made free from sin and death. Romans 8:2 shows us the miserable condition of all persons by nature, as well as the happy recovery and restoration of believers by grace.[12]

It is the excellence and commendation of artists to show their skill where bunglers fail. This is observable and remarkable in God himself. He first takes notice of the weakness and insufficiency which is in us, and then delights to express and put forth his own power and skillfulness. He does that in this Scripture (Rom. 8:3). To free us from condemnation, God found a way: sending his own Son into the world for our redemption. See, then, the defect implied (on our part) and the defect supplied (by God's grace).[13]

There were two things which God especially aimed at in sending Christ into the world: the satisfying of his own glorious attributes (his justice and mercy) and the procuring of our salvation—and so, his glory and our good—the fulfillment of his law and provision for our own good.[14]

According to Romans 8:5, there is a radical difference between the flesh and the Spirit. There is nothing more necessary for a Christian than to understand his spiritual condition: what he is by reason of sin, and the corruption of man through the Fall—and what he is by the virtue of grace, and the recovery of his Fall in Christ… From different principles come different actions and operations… They that are after the flesh mind the things of the flesh, but the Spirit-led follow the things of the Spirit.[15]

Romans 8:6 states the matter clearly. There is not a greater difference between good and bad men in their principles, than there is also in their conditions, nor in the things which come from them, and are done by them, than in the things which happen to them or are done upon them. Consider the contrast between life and death, happiness and misery, peace and eternal destruction.[16]

Romans 8:7 underlines the fact that ignorance and disobedience of

God's law is deadly. Indeed, they are worse than death. Whatsoever is enmity against God must, of necessity, be worse. Mind, will and affections are adversely affected. Consider what evil there is in such enmity against God. Let us also judge and estimate, and take account of ourselves, and see how far we are God's friends.[17]

They that are in the flesh cannot please God. Romans 8:8 is as powerful as it is plain. Carnal-mindedness... is a business in which all men by nature are carried and addicted... They are not subject to the law of God, nor indeed can be. Neither can they please God... They are in no way acceptable to him, but deserve to be cast out of his presence... Conversion begins when we see the vileness and sinfulness of our nature, and the misery to which we are subject.[18]

Christ's people, however, are not directed or dominated by the flesh, but are indwelt by the Spirit who creates true spirituality.[19] The Spirit dwells in the children of God, who are not carnal but spiritual. Even the best of God's servants must cope with the remainder of corruption in this present life. Yet they are not led away by it, for the Spirit dwells in them as temples of the living God (1 Cor. 3:16-17; 6:19-20).[20]

Don't pamper the body, but enjoy the life of grace and glory (2 Cor. 4:17; Ps. 73:26). Look beyond the dissolution of the body to a new body made by God in heaven (2 Cor. 5:1).[21]

Believers may draw comfort against the fears and terrors of death because the Spirit who raised Jesus from the dead will also quicken our mortal bodies. Romans 8:11 assures us of this. Death is neither total nor perpetual. Because Christ lives, we too shall live (John 14:19). He is risen to manifest the completeness of the redemption which he wrought for us, declaring us absolved and acquitted in the sight and presence of God. He lives by the power of God, and so shall we. It makes much for the honour and dignity of the Servant of God, that he whom the heaven of heavens could not contain should take up his residence in such narrow rooms as our hearts, and make us an habitation to himself through his Spirit.[22]

Romans 8:12 tells us that we are not debtors to the flesh but owe everything to the Spirit who sanctifies and enlivens our souls... furnishing us with grace here and glory hereafter. So let us lead holy lives, owing him everything. We are bankrupts and beggars and desperadoes. And we must admit, as our Saviour himself has taught us to say, we are unprofitable servants, we have only done that which was our duty to do (Luke 17:10).[23]

Shun the ways of the flesh, and walk in the ways of the Spirit. The former lifestyle is destined to death, but the latter—though involving the mortification of the deeds of the body—leads to life.

Romans 8:13 states this without ambiguity. One way ends in punishment, the other is rewarded with life (Rom. 6:23). Drunkards, gluttons, wantons, and other intemperate persons are self-destructive. They deprive themselves of grace, holiness, peace, and spiritual comfort, while exposing themselves to God's wrath for defacing the divine image. The doctrines of threatening or warning do well agree with the preaching of the gospel. There is nothing more necessary for people than that they should sometimes hear of hell. Such dreadful intimation may move them to repentance and new obedience.[24]

Children of God

Romans 8:14 identifies the people of God as those who are led by the Spirit of God. Adoption by him brings us into his family. Because we belong, we need to imitate and resemble him who is our Father—his purity and sanctity. Mind, will, and affections are to be guided by the Spirit, if we would be more like our Father. We also need to respond aright to the diversity of God's children, since we share the same gracious workings, the same love of God, the same hatred of sin.[25]

God's children have not received the spirit of bondage that leads to fear, but they have been given the Spirit of adoption which puts them in a most intimate relationship with the Father (Rom. 8:15). The text contains a negative as well as a positive proposition, contrasting the spirit of bondage and the Spirit of adoption. The former brings fear, the latter draws near to the Father with confidence. The former results from the ministry of the law, and the latter that of the gospel.[26]

We have every assurance of being children of God when the Spirit bears witness with our spirit that we belong to the Father's family (Rom. 8:16). The Spirit bears testimony that is true regarding our adoption into the Father's family (John 1:12). Because we are his children, he has sent forth the Spirit of his Son into our hearts (Gal. 4:4-7).[27]

If we are God's children, then we are heirs of God and joint heirs with Christ (Rom. 8:17). We partake of a blessed estate, in the Father's house of many mansions. If we are his children, we are his heirs. No good thing will God withhold from them that walk uprightly. They shall be blest with grace and glory (Ps. 84:11)—grace considered as the means, and glory as the end of all God has promised his people. Nowhere in Scripture is salvation considered as a matter of merit.

Present sufferings and future glory

If we are joint heirs with Christ, we may also suffer with him and then be glorified together with him. Together, we share present sufferings and future glory (1 Peter 1:7; 4:12).[28]

The apostle continues his teaching on sufferings and the glory to be revealed in Romans 8:18. We are kept from dejection and despondency in seasons of affliction if we remember God's promise of an incomparable glory yet to be revealed in his people—a glory they had supposed lost in time of trouble and affliction (2 Cor. 4:17–5:3).[29]

Present sufferings are not worthy to be compared with future glory. Romans 8:19 tells us that the created universe waits with earnest expectation for the manifestation—the glorious revelation—of God's children. This will be consummated at the day of Christ's return. Then shall the tares be bundled and burned, but the righteous shall shine forth as the sun in the kingdom of their Father (Matt. 13:42-43; 25:32-33).[30]

Romans 8:20 contrasts the creation subjected to vanity, unwillingly, with the hope of God's children. The world is marked by emptiness, insufficiency, transiency, uncertainty, and mortality. But to his people, God gives hope.

The apostle Peter, speaking of Paul's epistles, says that there are some things in them which are hard to be understood. Romans 8:21, says Horton, is one of them (2 Peter 3:16). He calls it a very difficult Scripture and calls on the assistance of the Holy Spirit of God, who alone has the key for the unlocking and opening of it to us. Somehow, creation itself shall be delivered by God from the bondage of corruption. It shall reflect the glorious liberty of the children of God. When? When the risen Christ returns and his glory is revealed (Phil. 3:21; 1 Cor. 15:43; Rev. 21:4).[31]

Those who are now troubled with pains and aches, filled with sores and ulcers, deprived of limbs and senses, or [afflicted with] deformity or imperfection, shall experience change. Those who do not partake of a gracious liberty in this world, however, shall never be partakers of a glorious liberty in the world to come. It is the liberty of the children of God, and of none other, which is here spoken of.[32]

According to Romans 8:22, the whole creation groans and travails in pain until now. And not only that, but we ourselves also sense this. Passion and compassion are both felt in the great disorder and confusion of all things here below, so that creation grieves and groans.[33] Yet God has given us his Spirit, with graces and comforts in this present life and glory in the world to come. We wait for "the adoption, the redemption of our body." Ahead is the glorious manifestation of the children of God and their future deliverance from the bondage of corruption. This is a doctrine of very great importance and influence. While we wait with patience for that consummation, we aim at the glory of God, the good of the church, the flourishing of piety and religion in the times and places where we live.[34]

We are saved by hope, as well as faith. Paul writes that we hope for what is yet to come, and that we wait with patience for it.

Believers are already adopted into God's family, made heirs, and indwelt by the Spirit, but expect their further redemption—the resurrection of the body—in another world. Our present salvation lies not so much in possession as it does in expectation. If we have this hope in us, we must purify ourselves even as Christ is pure (1 John 3:3). So shall we be strengthened by assurance and evidence, holding firmly to the hope of salvation, the hope of eternal life, the hope of glory (1 Thess. 5:8; Titus 1:2; Col. 1:27). Since we are saved in hope, it concerns us... to keep hope alive in ourselves.[35]

Romans 8:26 reminds us that the Spirit helps us in our infirmities, making intercessions for us with groanings which cannot be uttered. We need such assistance to endure afflictions and sufferings in this present life. Success in this business is full of hardship and difficulty, but we should remember that Christ accompanies us in our suffering (Rom. 8:17) and that the result of such sufferings is incomparable glory (Rom. 8:18). And in all this, we are upheld by the intercession of the Spirit, who heals those weaknesses and infirmities which are in us. He helps us against corruptions (to avoid them) and assists us with reference to duties (that we may perform them). Our infirmities may be many, but our Helper is mighty.[36]

The God who searches our hearts knows what is the mind of the Spirit. He makes intercession for the saints, according to the will of God. We have a great privilege and advantage in our prayers to God at the throne of grace, since the Spirit promotes and furthers them. God knows the hearts of his children, and the Spirit knows the Father's will (1 John 5:14-15). In our prayers we must pray according to his will. That which is contrary to God's commanding will can never be agreeable to his approving will.[37]

Romans 8:28 is one of the most quoted passages of Scripture. We need comfort against the bitterness of the cross and the afflictions incident to our lives. But do we love God, and are we among those who have been called according to his purposes?

God wills the good of his children. All the attributes of God, all the offices of Christ, all the gifts and graces of the Spirit combine for the good of them that belong to him. All the three persons in the Trinity cooperate in the good of God's elect.

It is a great part of skill and faithfulness in those who are ministers of the gospel and stewards of the mysteries of Christ (1 Cor. 4:1) to distribute to all kinds of persons that portion which is fittest for them and properly appertains to them. As our Saviour puts it, negatively, we are not to give holy things to dogs, nor cast pearls before swine. God's comfort and consolation are for such as love him and have responded to his call. Christian affection and effectual vocation are conditions not to be neglected. There can be no assurance without them.

To love God is to esteem him highly, desire fellowship with him, and delight in him. It also involves zeal for him and the willingness to part with anything for him (Matt. 22:37-38).

God's eternal purpose and grace

To be called according to his purposes is to respond when the Spirit speaks through the Word, effectually calling the elect from ignorance and unbelief to true knowledge and faith in Christ. It is the acceptation of his invitation (Matt. 11:28; John 1:11-12).

Romans 8:29 deals with foreknowledge, predestination, conformity to the image of God's Son, and Christ's preeminence among many brethren. This follows the truths mentioned in the preceding verse and relates to God's immutable decree and his sovereign grace. Consider first, God's eternal purpose and decree concerning his children: whom he did foreknow, he did predestinate; secondly, the end in view: to be conformed to the image of his Son; thirdly, the limitation of this conformity of the saints to Christ: that he might be the first-born among many brethren.[38]

God loves his people from all eternity, as expressed in his foreknowledge, election, and predestination, appointing them to the attaining of everlasting salvation. This doctrine was taught by Christ, then by his apostles, then by ministers and teachers in the course of church history. Our salvation is secure, founded on God's eternal purpose and divine decree. Rather than argue about election and predestination, we must be willing to repent and believe, embrace the gospel, and receive Christ on his own terms and conditions, doing what he requires of us.

Romans 8:30 continues the apostle's line of thought: foreknowledge, election, predestination—and now, vocation, justification and glorification. These are links in the "golden chain" of our salvation. Already, vocation has been discussed when dealing with Romans 8:28. All who are effectually called have been from all eternity elected and pre-ordained to eternal salvation. Then we come to justification—a term to be taken in a judicial (or forensic) signification: declaring one to be just, and absolving him from condemnation. So, the justified are acquitted and taken for righteous in God's sight (Acts 13:38-39). Christ has paid their debts, endured their penalty and clothed them with his own righteousness.[39]

The justified are also numbered among the glorified: to be with Christ and like Christ. These links of salvation's "golden chain" also relate to the doctrine of final perseverance. God's children cannot fall from grace, or be excluded from the kingdom of heaven (John 10:28-29). The whole work of salvation, from top to bottom, and eternity to eternity, wholly belongs to God and proceeds from the abundant riches of his grace. He has foreknown, predestinated, called, justified, and glorified (Rom. 11:36).

In Romans 8:31, the apostle uses questions to express conclusions—what Horton calls: an "Introductory Preface" and a "Peremptory Expostulation." Since these truths have been affirmed, how ought we to live? And, if God be for us—since he has expressed his everlasting love and shown himself to be for us—we have a most blessed assurance.[40]

The God of the covenant offers his people protection (as to the avoiding of evil) and provisions (as to the enjoyment of good), so that believers are assured of his fatherly care. Romans 8:32 reminds us of God's love in giving his beloved Son in sacrifice for the good, comfort, and salvation of his elect (John 3:16; 1 John

4:9). What are we willing to part with for his sake? How will they part with their relationships for Christ, who will not part with their corrupting associates? How will they part with their lives for Christ, who are unwilling to part with their lusts?[41]

Our assurance is further made firm by the fact that our sins have been pardoned. God declares us justified—acquitted and absolved—if we are numbered among his elect. In Romans 8:30 we see that election passes through effectual calling to justification. Now, in Romans 8:33, the apostle goes from justification back to election. Our justification involves the remission and forgiveness of sins, and the imputation of Christ's righteousness, so that we are graciously and mercifully welcomed into God's family.[42]

Romans 8:34 assures believers that they are free from condemnation when they are rightly related to the risen, ascended, and enthroned Christ who intercedes on their behalf. There is no such lovely and glorious sight in all the world, as of a Christian in the full sail and flight of faith, wherein he carries all before him, and triumphs over everything that seems to stand in opposition against him—the evil of punishment or the evil of sins.[43]

The apostle moves from triumphing over sin (which is the sting of every affliction) to triumphing over affliction itself. It cannot separate us from the love of Christ according to Romans 8:35. Indeed, believers are beloved of Christ and accepted of the Father through the Son (Eph. 1:6). Not even the sword of persecution or violent death can separate Christ's sheep from their Shepherd (Rom. 8:36). They endure with patience and show fidelity in their persecutions and tribulations. In all these adversities, they are more than conquerors through him who loved—and continues to love—his people.[44]

Romans 8:37 describes such martyrs as being more than conquerors. This is the happy privilege of all true believers. Every good Christian is a victor and a conqueror, entitled to eat of the tree of life and have an honourable place in the temple of God (Rev. 2:7; 3:12; 21:7).[45]

In Romans 8:38-39, the apostle Paul concludes with a fresh

supply of triumphant expressions. He is firmly persuaded that nothing shall ever separate believers from the love of God revealed in Jesus Christ. They shall be infinitely and transcendently glorious.[46]

Chapter 14

Advent to judgement

Some speculate that the European Union is really a revived Roman Empire, some wonder regarding the identity of the Anti-Christ, others prognosticate about thousands of horsemen coming from Russia invading Israel to plunder its secret oil reserves, while others make predictions about popes and politicians who may fit the designation of 666. But one thing is sure: God has set a day when he will judge the world with justice by the risen Christ. In view of that inevitable encounter, repentance should be at the very top of everyone's agenda (Acts 17:30-31).

Preparing for Christ's return

David Dickson (1583-1662), who served as a pastor and professor in Scotland, wrote not only a voluminous commentary on the Psalms, but an exposition of most of the New Testament epistles. His comments confirm the view that the Puritans did not abuse Bible prophecy for date-setting speculation, but related eschatology to ethics and evangelism.

Dickson declares that the night of ignorance and darkness is past (Romans 13:11-14). We face a new state of illumination. A future glory approaches. Let us, therefore, put on the armour of light, that we may withstand the devil, and the world… Let us walk honestly, as in the day, as becomes the children of light, regenerate through the grace of the gospel… putting off all that pollutes and corrupts, but putting on the Lord Jesus Christ—so that his righteousness may cover our nakedness.[1]

The Philippian letter (Phil. 3:20-21) also relates character to the consummation. Paul says that our heavenly connection prepares us for the Lord's return. We look for the return of the Christ at the last day, not as a judge who will condemn us, but as our Saviour, who will perfectly accomplish our salvation. Although our bodies are now corruptible, vile, and miserable, yet Christ will hereafter thoroughly change them… and free them from corruption. He will make our bodies conformable unto his glorious body… adorned with glorious qualities, by his power and efficacy. He can destroy death and the grave, and is able to endow our bodies with whatever qualities he pleases.[2]

According to Colossians 3:1-4, God's elect are already spiritually risen with Christ. They should, then, set their sights on those things that are above, where Christ is at God's right hand. Their life—their adoption, their righteousness, their inheritance, their sanctification and glorification—is hidden from the world. But when Christ (who is our life) shall appear, then shall they also appear with him in glory, brought forth in the sight of men and angels. All this… when Christ shall be manifested in his second coming. Therefore, let us mortify our old nature (fornication, uncleanness, inordinate affections, concupiscence and idolatrous covetousness, anger, wrath, malice, blasphemy, filthy communication) and in place of these vices put on Christ-like virtues (Col. 3:5-11). This is the way to prepare for our Lord's glorious return.[3]

In 1 Thessalonians, Christians are described as people who have renounced idolatry and wait for God's Son from heaven—the One whom God raised from the dead, even Jesus, who delivered them from the wrath to come. He, the Redeemer, dead and risen for us, shall come from heaven, a Judge to destroy all unbelievers and to deliver his own (1 Thess. 1:9-10).

The return of Christ is connected with the resurrection of the dead (1 Thess. 4:13-18).[4] Dickson mentions that the apostle's aim is to offer believers consolation against the immoderate mourning that belongs to heathens and infidels who have no hope of (a blessed) resurrection. If we are certain in our belief that Christ is risen from the dead, we should also be certain that the faithful dead in Christ shall rise again and be presented alive in the company of Christ at the day of judgement. This consolation is made strong by revelation from the Lord. Paul foretells the manner of the coming of Christ and the resurrection in six statements:

1. The faithful who are alive at the coming of Christ shall not be resurrected prior to those that are dead in Christ.
2. Christ shall descend from heaven with his holy angels, with authority and majesty.
3. The supreme Judge, he shall command that every element give up its dead. All shall be gathered before his tribunal.
4. Before those still alive on the earth shall be changed, the dead in Christ shall arise.
5. The faithful who are alive at the coming of the Lord, being changed suddenly in a moment, in the twinkling of an eye, from mortality to immortality, shall be caught up with the saints that are raised, to meet the Lord in the air.
6. After the judgement, the saints shall go with the Lord into heaven and shall remain with him to eternity. Paul says nothing here regarding the reprobate, because his consolation does not pertain to them. Nor can any comfort be taken for them when they die. But let believers comfort one another with these words.

Again, consider what the apostle says in 1 Thessalonians 5:1-11. The time and hour of the Lord's coming is not revealed, but lies hidden in the secrets of God. Nor is it expedient to inquire curiously concerning it. But the day of the Lord will come as a thief in the night, suddenly and by surprise. Believers, however, should not fear that day, because they are not in the darkness of sin and ignorance. They are children of light, of the day, not existing in the bondage of ignorance and sin. In view of all this, we should show watchfulness and sobriety, and so face that day without fear. We are to study moderation in all things and earnestly endeavour after works of holiness. Our lives should be characterized by faith, hope, and love, remembering that Christians ought to live as in a warfare... God has not predestinated us to wrath, but to obtain salvation by our Lord Jesus Christ. So, let us steer clear of indulgence in disobedience, deserving of God's wrath. Let us, therefore, strive unto salvation in the ways of the Lord. He died for us that we should live together with him... in the works of holiness.[5]

Writing to the Corinthians, the apostle reminds everyone that we must all appear before the judgement seat of Christ (2 Cor. 5:10). Punishment shall be inflicted upon the wicked, but rewards are in prospect for those whose sins are pardoned and whose works are good.[6]

The motivation for godly living provided by the promise of Christ's return comes with stunning force in Titus 2:11-14. Dickson notes that the hope of Christ's return is a powerful stimulous to the performance of the duties we owe to others. Renewed and reconciled, we not only hold dear the doctrine of saving grace but take seriously the precepts of Scripture.[7]

Since the gospel of the grace of God has offered salvation to all kinds of people, it is appropriate that people of all sorts show their thankfulness to God in a holy lifestyle. The gospel not only teaches us what duties we are bound to perform, but also instructs us how to draw strength from the fountain of the grace of Christ, from his death and resurrection, so that we deny ungodliness and worldly lusts, and live soberly (as to ourselves), justly (as to our neighbours), and holy (as to God). Why do this? Because we expect eternal life at the coming of Christ, who is the great God, one with the Father and the Holy Spirit, and our Saviour. He gave himself for us, that he might effectually redeem us from the bondage of sin and purchase us to himself as his own possession, that we might follow after good works. Unless we would have that redemption void in our lives, we must of necessity forsake our sins and follow after the virtues that belong to newness of life.[8]

In 2 Timothy, after that reassuring reference to the authority and utility of the Holy Spirit (2 Tim. 3:15-17), Paul seriously exhorts his young associate to discharge his responsibilities faithfully. This exhortation, declares Dickson, involves five duties: diligence in preaching; striving against all impediments; sparing no effort in service; encouraging people to make progress in the faith and obedience of Christ; mixing his reproofs with zeal and fervour, seasoned with gentleness, lest his labour be in vain. This charge comes in the context of the majesty of God, the presence of Christ, the judgement seat of our Lord, and the royal appearing of him who shall judge the living and the dead. This righteous Judge shall bestow a crown of righteousness on all who love his appearing, at the day of his return (2 Tim. 4:1,8).[9]

The author of the letter to the Hebrews reminds his readers that it is appointed to everyone once to die and after this to face the judgement. Once did Christ offer himself as a sacrifice for the sins of many. But now, risen from the dead, he shall appear a second time—without the humiliation and suffering of his first appearing—unto salvation. He shall return to judge both the living and the dead. At that day of judgement, he shall appear in glory (Heb. 9:27-28).[10]

The apostle Peter encourages elders to feed and govern the flock of God, confident that when the Chief Shepherd shall appear, they shall receive from him a crown of unfading glory (1 Peter 5:1-4).[11] And the apostle John also emphasizes the relationship between ethics and eschatology. After referring to the Father's love in making us his children, he prophesies that when Christ shall return we shall be transformed into his likeness, for we shall see him as he is. This lively hope should be a powerful incentive to purify ourselves. The pattern in this purifying process is none other than the returning Redeemer (1 John 3:1-3).[12]

The Scriptures—whether historical, prophetical, poetical or moral—were not given to stir up contention but to bring us correction and comfort. The general scope of the Scriptures is our edification in faith and obedience, by promises, precepts, and examples, so that we in all our tribulations—patiently obeying the will of God—might have consolation and hope through the Scriptures (Rom. 15:4).[13]

Wicked scoffers will ridicule the promise of Christ's return. But the day of his coming will come. If it seems delayed, it is only because God is not willing that any should perish, but that all should come to repentance. Nevertheless, the Lord will come like a thief in the night, overtaking scoffers unawares. The whole universe shall be affected, as the elements melt with a great noise and burning heat. In view of all this, what sort of persons should we be? Ought we not to prepare by pursuing holiness? The apostle Peter says that all who hope for Christ's return should labour patiently in their vocation, and endeavour after godliness.[14]

A glorious hope

Joseph Caryl's (1602-1673) multi-volume *Exposition of the Book of Job* was published in London in 1676. An abridged form was produced by John Berrie in Edinburgh in 1836. From that version we get a foretaste of our glorious hope as revealed in Job 19:23-27.

Suffering and sorrowful, Job cried out to his friends for pity... Now he begs their attention and a serious consideration of what he has to say: a strong profession of his faith in the Redeemer, and of a happy resurrection to a better life... Job was not only willing to be tested by men, but also to appear before God.

Caryl calls faith a shield whereby we may quench all the fiery darts of the wicked (Eph. 6:16). By faith in the Redeemer, Job waits for the resurrection of his body to eternal life, after death has done its worst. With undoubted certainty, without wavering, he affirms the resurrection of the Redeemer and the conviction that his body shall be raised again.

Saints do not see what they believe, but they know what they believe... Such knowledge, like faith, is the gift of God. We see our Redeemer buying back that which was alienated and paying a ransom, not by force, rescuing prisoners. Job speaks of Christ as the Prince of Life. In contrast to mortal, dying creatures, he lives... he has all life in himself. All the life creatures enjoy is bestowed by him.

Afflictions do not separate from Christ... A believer may attain to the full assurance of his participation in Christ, knowing that his Redeemer lives... It is incumbent on all believers to love Christ and live for him, who not only lives for their good, but shares his life with them. He shall stand at the latter day upon the earth... These words are to be understood of his second coming, when he will raise the dead and proceed to judgement at the last day. The resurrection of the body shall be effected by the power of Christ. Death itself is under the dominion of the Lord of life. We read of a two-fold resurrection effected by this power. All are by nature dead in sin, but when we hear the voice of Christ, speaking by his Word and Spirit, we come to life: a new birth, a new life, a resurrection. But all shall hear his voice and come forth from the grave at the end, when he comes to minister judgement to all. The Redeemer himself shall be the judge... What can be more terrible than to be judged by a Redeemer whose grace and mercy we have refused?

Having confessed his faith in the Redeemer, Job now expresses his confidence regarding his own personal resurrection... He believes that he shall see God, for himself: "I shall have a glorified eye to see a glorified Saviour."[15]

Caryl says that our souls, like our bodies, must be changed before they can be fit for glory. He adds: "I shall see God as a friend, ready to receive me into his everlasting embrace." The faith of a blessed resurrection comforts and supports us under the afflictions of this life (Job 19:23-27).[16]

The Great Commission

The approaching end of the world was related by the Puritans to the church's mission, as well as to the return of Christ, the resurrection of the body, and the judgement of all mankind. An influential voice regarding the Great Commission was that of Peter Martyr Vermigli. In expounding Romans 9 to 11, he noted the plan of God, in his sovereign grace, to lead both believing Jews and Gentiles into one body of Christ. They were to be invited, without partiality, into the kingdom of grace preparatory to the return of Christ and the kingdom of glory. This was the Puritan hope.[17]

As Christ would have us be certainly persuaded that there shall be a day of judgement, both to deter all men from sin and for the greater consolation of the godly in their adversity, so will he have that day unknown to men, that they may shake off all carnal security and be always watchful, because they know not at what hour the Lord will come; and be ever prepared to say, "Come, Lord Jesus, come quickly. Amen."[18]

Endnotes

Foreword

1   See his William Laud, *A Speech delivered in the Star-Chamber...at the Censure, of John Bastwick, Henry Burton, & William Prinn; Concerning pretended Innovations in the Church* in *The Works of...William Laud* (Oxford: John Henry Parker, 1857), VI/I, 57.
2   That they did not thereby neglect the importance of the Table can be seen from Chapter 10 below. But for the Puritans the Word had a higher priority.
3   John Cheeseman, *The Priority of Preaching* (Edinburgh/Carlisle, Pennsylvania: The Banner of Truth Trust, 2006), 9.
4   See Cheeseman, *Priority of Preaching*, 8.

Introduction

1   G.C. Curteis, *Dissent in its Relation to the Church of England* (London: Macmillan, 1872), 86.
2   Curteis, *Dissent in its Relation to the Church of England*, 104.
3   Curteis, *Dissent in its Relation to the Church of England*, 142.
4   Philip Schaff, *The Creeds of Christendom*, 3 vols. (New York: Harper & Brothers, 1877), 1:703
5   T.D. Lea, "The Hermeneutics of the Puritans" in the *Journal of Evangelical Theology* (vol. 39, no. 2, June 1996), 276.
6   Lea, "The Hermeneutics of the Puritans," 284.
7   Schaff, *The Creeds of Christendom*, 1:704.

Chapter 1: The infallible Word

1   John Owen, *The Reason of Faith* (London, 1677. Repr. Glasgow, 1801), vii.
2   Owen, *Reason of Faith*, 11.
3   Owen, *Reason of Faith*, 36.
4   Owen, *Reason of Faith*, 37

5   Owen, *Reason of Faith*, 40.
6   Owen, *Reason of Faith*, 78.
7   Owen, *Reason of Faith*, 83.
8   Owen, *Reason of Faith*, 85.
9   Owen, *Reason of Faith*, 92.
10 Owen, *Reason of Faith*, 132-133.
11 Owen, *Reason of Faith*, 144.
12 Owen, *Reason of Faith*, 183.
13 Owen, *Reason of Faith*, 232.
14 Owen, *Reason of Faith*, 240.
15 Owen, *Reason of Faith*, 255.
16 Owen, *Reason of Faith*, 313-314.
17 William Pemble, *Works* (London, 1635), 28.
18 Pemble, *Works*, 83.
19 Pemble, *Works*, 94.

Chapter 2: No upstart sect

1   John Owen, *The Works of John Owen*, 24 vols., ed. William H. Goold (London, 1851), 2:377-439. The Banner of Truth Trust (Edinburgh) has reprinted this edition.
2   Owen, *Works*, 2:379.
3   Owen, *Works*, 2:479.
4   Owen, *Works*, 2:480.
5   Owen, *Works*, 2:381.
6   Owen, *Works*, 2:382.
7   Owen, *Works*, 2:398.
8   James Durham, *The Ten Commandments* (Edinburgh, 1676), 8.
9   Durham, *The Ten Commandments*, 5.
10 Durham, *The Ten Commandments*, 185.
11 Durham, *The Ten Commandments*, 237.
12 Durham, *The Ten Commandments*, 334.
13 Durham, *The Ten Commandments*, 364.
14 *An Exposition of the Symbole or Creed of the Apostles* in *The Works of William Perkins* (Cambridge: J. Legat, 1603).
15 *Westminster Shorter Catechism* (London, 1647), Q. 98-107.

Chapter 3: The Messiah revealed

1   Thomas Watson, *Practical Divinity: The Shorter Catechism* (Philadelphia, 1833), 113.
2   Watson, *Practical Divinity: The Shorter Catechism*, 114.
3   Watson, *Practical Divinity: The Shorter Catechism*, 115-116.
4   John Flavel, *The Fountain of Life* (London, 1820), 96-97.
5   Flavel, *The Fountain of Life*, 104-105.

6   Richard Sibbes, *The Complete Works of Richard Sibbes*, 7 vols. (Edinburgh, 1862), 2:140. The Banner of Truth Trust (Edinburgh) has reprinted this edition.
7   Watson, *Practical Divinity: The Shorter Catechism*, 117.
8   Watson, *Practical Divinity: The Shorter Catechism*, 117.
9   Watson, *Practical Divinity: The Shorter Catechism*, 118-119.
10 Watson, *Practical Divinity: The Shorter Catechism*, 121.
11 Watson, *Practical Divinity: The Shorter Catechism*, 122.
12 Watson, *Practical Divinity: The Shorter Catechism*, 124.
13 Flavel, *The Fountain of Life*, 180-181.
14 Watson, *Practical Divinity: The Shorter Catechism*, 126-127.
15 Watson, *Practical Divinity: The Shorter Catechism*, 129.
16 Watson, *Practical Divinity: The Shorter Catechism*, 129.

Chapter 4: Pastoral ministry

1   William Gouge, *The Works of William Gouge*, 2 vols. (London: John Beale, 1627), 2:245.
2   Gouge, *Works*, 2:246.
3   Gouge, *Works*, 2:247.
4   Gouge, *Works*, 2:248.
5   Gouge, *Works*, 2:249.
6   Gouge, *Works*, 2:250.
7   Gouge, *Works*, 2:251.
8   Gouge, *Works*, 2:254.
9   Gouge, *Works*, 2:255.
10 Gouge, *Works*, 2:256.
11 Gouge, *Works*, 2:257.
12 Gouge, *Works*, 2:258.
13 Gougc, *Works*, 2:260.
14 Gouge, *Works*, 2:260-261.
15 Gouge, *Works*, 2:261.
16 Gouge, *Works*, 2:262.
17 Gouge, *Works*, 2:263.
18 Gouge, *Works*, 2:264.
19 Gouge, *Works*, 2:265.
20 Gouge, *Works*, 2:267.
21 Gouge, *Works*, 2:270.
22 Gouge, *Works*, 2:280.
23 John Owen, *The Works of John Owen*, 24 vols., ed. William H. Goold (London, 1851), 9:445.
24 Owen, *Works*, 9:455.
25 Owen, *Works*, 9:457-458.
26 Owen, *Works*, 9:458-459.
27 Owen, *Works*, 9:439.

Chapter 5: Guilt and grace

1 Arthur Hildersam, *CLII lectures upon Psalme LI* [or *One-Hundred-and-Fifty-Two Lectures on Psalm 51*] (London, 1642), 7-8.
2 Hildersam, *Psalm 51*, 17-18.
3 Hildersam, *Psalm 51*, 30-31.
4 Hildersam, *Psalm 51*, 45-47.
5 Hildersam, *Psalm 51*, 54-55.
6 Hildersam, *Psalm 51*, 58.
7 Hildersam, *Psalm 51*, 79-81.
8 Hildersam, *Psalm 51*, 93-94.
9 Hildersam, *Psalm 51*, 103.
10 Hildersam, *Psalm 51*, 126.
11 Hildersam, *Psalm 51*, 138.
12 Hildersam, *Psalm 51*, 142-144.
13 Hildersam, *Psalm 51*, 152-160.
14 Hildersam, *Psalm 51*, 181-187.
15 Hildersam, *Psalm 51*, 226-246.
16 Hildersam, *Psalm 51*, 269-273.
17 Hildersam, *Psalm 51*, 357-358.
18 Hildersam, *Psalm 51*, 436-437.
19 Hildersam, *Psalm 51*, 549, 551.
20 Hildersam, *Psalm 51*, 725-727.

Chapter 6: The second birth

1 David Clarkson, "The New Creature" in *The Works of David Clarkson*, 3 vols. (Edinburgh: James Nichol, 1865), 2:6. The Banner of Truth Trust (Edinburgh) has reprinted this edition.
2 Clarkson, "The New Creature," 2:6.
3 Clarkson, "The New Creature," 2:7.
4 Clarkson, "The New Creature," 2:7-8.
5 Clarkson, "The New Creature," 2:10.
6 Clarkson, "The New Creature," 2:11.
7 Clarkson, "The New Creature," 2:13.
8 Clarkson, "The New Creature," 2:14.
9 Clarkson, "The New Creature," 2:15.
10 Clarkson, "The New Creature," 2:17.
11 Clarkson, "The New Creature," 2:18.
12 Clarkson, "The New Creature," 2:19.
13 Clarkson, "The New Creature," 2:20.
14 Clarkson, "The New Creature," 2:21.
15 Clarkson, "The New Creature," 2:22.
16 Clarkson, "The New Creature," 2:23.

17 Clarkson, "The New Creature," 2:24.
18 Clarkson, "The New Creature," 2:25.
19 Clarkson, "The New Creature," 2:26.
20 Clarkson, "The New Creature," 2:27.

Chapter 7: Radical repentance

1 David Clarkson, *The Works of David Clarkson*, 3 vols. (Edinburgh: James Nichol, 1865), 1:16-18.
2 Clarkson, *Works*, 1:19-20.
3 Clarkson, *Works*, 1:19-21.
4 Clarkson, *Works*, 1:23-24.
5 Clarkson, *Works*, 1:25.
6 Clarkson, *Works*, 1:27-28.
7 Clarkson, *Works*, 1:35.
8 Clarkson, *Works*, 1:41-42.
9 Clarkson, *Works*, 1:43-45.
10 Clarkson, *Works*, 1:59-60.
11 Richard Sibbes, *The Complete Works of Richard Sibbes*, 7 vols. (Edinburgh, 1862), 1:184.
12 Sibbes, *Works*, 2:277.
13 Sibbes, *Works*, 2:305.
14 Sibbes, *Works*, 2:306.
15 Sibbes, *Works*, 2:306.
16 *Westminster Shorter Catechism* (London, 1647), Q. 87.

Chapter 8: Justified and sanctified

1 John Owen, *The Works of John Owen*, 24 vols., ed. William H. Goold (London, 1851), 5:7-8.
2 Owen, *Works*, 5:9-10.
3 Owen, *Works*, 5:12.
4 Owen, *Works*, 5:13.
5 Owen, *Works*, 5:17-18.
6 Owen, *Works*, 5:20.
7 Owen, *Works*, 5:21,23.
8 Owen, *Works*, 5:25.
9 Owen, *Works*, 5:27-30.
10 Owen, *Works*, 5:31,33.
11 Owen, *Works*, 5:34.
12 Owen, *Works*, 5:41.
13 Owen, *Works*, 5:48.
14 Owen, *Works*, 5:52-54.
15 Owen, *Works*, 5:62.

16 Owen, *Works*, 5:65.
17 Owen, *Works*, 5:67.
18 Owen, *Works*, 5:67.
19 Owen, *Works*, 5:290-291.
20 Owen, *Works*, 5:291.
21 Owen, *Works*, 5:291-292.
22 Owen, *Works*, 5:293.
23 Owen, *Works*, 5:293.
24 Owen, *Works*, 5:294.
25 Owen, *Works*, 5:294.
26 Owen, *Works*, 5:295.
27 Owen, *Works*, 5:295.
28 Owen, *Works*, 5:295.
29 Owen, *Works*, 5:296.
30 Owen, *Works*, 5:296.
31 Owen, *Works*, 5:297.
32 Owen, *Works*, 5:297.
33 Owen, *Works*, 5:298.

Chapter 9: Spiritual conflict

1 William Gouge, *The Works of William Gouge*, 2 vols. (London, 1627), 2:3
2 Gouge, *Works*, 2:4.
3 Gouge, *Works*, 2:5.
4 Gouge, *Works*, 2:6.
5 Gouge, *Works*, 2:6.
6 Gouge, *Works*, 2:7.
7 Gouge, *Works*, 2:10-11.
8 Gouge, *Works*, 2:11.
9 Gouge, *Works*, 2:14-15.
10 Gouge, *Works*, 2:15-16.
11 Gouge, *Works*, 2:17-18.
12 Gouge, *Works*, 2:19-20.
13 Gouge, *Works*, 2:23-24.
14 Gouge, *Works*, 2:25-26.
15 Gouge, *Works*, 2:27.
16 Gouge, *Works*, 2:28-29.
17 Gouge, *Works*, 2:29-32.
18 Gouge, *Works*, 2:34-36.
19 Gouge, *Works*, 2:41.
20 Gouge, *Works*, 2:46.
21 Gouge, *Works*, 2:48-50.
22 Gouge, *Works*, 2:52-54.
23 Gouge, *Works*, 2:55-56.
24 Gouge, *Works*, 2:56-57.

25 Gouge, *Works*, 2:59.
26 Gouge, *Works*, 2:59-63.
27 Gouge, *Works*, 2:65.
28 Gouge, *Works*, 2:66-72.
29 Gouge, *Works*, 2:73-74.
30 Gouge, *Works*, 2:75-76.
31 Gouge, *Works*, 2:80-81.
32 Gouge, *Works*, 2:83.
33 Gouge, *Works*, 2:86-88.
34 Gouge, *Works*, 2:98-100.
35 Gouge, *Works*, 2:101-102.
36 Gouge, *Works*, 2:103-108.
37 Gouge, *Works*, 2:109-110.
38 Gouge, *Works*, 2:110-115.
39 Gouge, *Works*, 2:121-130.
40 Gouge, *Works*, 2:131-134.
41 Gouge, *Works*, 2:143-146.
42 Gouge, *Works*, 2:146-148.
43 Gouge, *Works*, 2:152-153.
44 Gouge, *Works*, 2:153-155.
45 Gouge, *Works*, 2:164-168.
46 William Gurnall, *The Christian in Complete Armour*, 2 vols. (London, 1655, 1662; repr., Edinburgh: The Banner of Truth Trust, 1964), 2:611.

Chapter 10: *Bread and wine*

1 William Tyndale, *An Answer to Sir Thomas More's Dialogue; The Supper of the Lord after the true meaning of John 6 and 1 Cor. 11* (Cambridge: Cambridge University Press, 1850), 218-268. This work was originally published in 1531.
2 Mariano Di Gangi, *Peter Martyr Vermigli: Renaissance Man, Reformation Master* (Lanham, MD: University Press of America, 1993).
3 Henry Smith, *The Sermons of Mr. Henry Smith* (London, 1675).
4 Smith, *Sermons*, 47.
5 Smith, *Sermons*, 55.
6 Smith, *Sermons*, 56-57.
7 Smith, *Sermons*, 57.
8 Smith, *Sermons*, 58.
9 Smith, *Sermons*, 60.
10 Smith, *Sermons*, 62.
11 Smith, *Sermons*, 69.
12 Smith, *Sermons*, 70.
13 John Owen, *The Works of John Owen*, 24 vols., ed. William H. Goold (London, 1851), 9:532.
14 Owen, *Works*, 9:534.
15 Owen, *Works*, 9:538, 539.

16 John Flavel, *The Fountain of Life* (London, 1820), 248.
17 Flavel, *The Fountain of Life*, 249.
18 Flavel, *The Fountain of Life*, 252.
19 Flavel, *The Fountain of Life*, 253.
20 Flavel, *The Fountain of Life*, 253.
21 Flavel, *The Fountain of Life*, 255.
22 Flavel, *The Fountain of Life*, 256.
23 Flavel, *The Fountain of Life*, 259.
24 Flavel, *The Fountain of Life*, 260.
25 Flavel, *The Fountain of Life*, 261.

Chapter 11: Renewal and reform

1 John Owen, *The Works of John Owen*, 24 vols., ed. William H. Goold (London, 1851), 1:433.
2 Owen, *Works*, 1:436.
3 Owen, *Works*, 1:441.
4 Owen, *Works*, 1:443.
5 Owen, *Works*, 1:445.
6 Owen, *Works*, 1:446.
7 Owen, *Works*, 1:447.
8 Owen, *Works*, 1:450.
9 Owen, *Works*, 1:452.
10 Owen, *Works*, 1:453.
11 Owen, *Works*, 1:456.
12 Owen, *Works*, 1:457.
13 Owen, *Works*, 1:459.
14 Owen, *Works*, 1:460.

Chapter 12: Family values

1 George Hutcheson, *An Exposition of the Gospel of Jesus Christ according to John* (London, 1657), 289-290, 292-293. The Banner of Truth Trust (Edinburgh) reprinted this edition in 1972.
2 Henry Smith, *The Sermons of Mr. Henry Smith* (London, 1675), 1-2.
3 Smith, *Sermons*, 2.
4 Smith, *Sermons*, 2.
5 Smith, *Sermons*, 19-21.
6 Smith, *Sermons*, 22.
7 Smith, *Sermons*, 23.
8 Smith, *Sermons*, 24.
9 Smith, *Sermons*, 25.
10 Smith, *Sermons*, 25.
11 Smith, *Sermons*, 32.
12 Edward Elton, *An Exposition of the Epistle of Saint Paul to the Colossians: Delivered*

in Sundry Sermons (London, 1620), 545-546.
  13 Elton, *Colossians*, 545-546.
  14 Elton, *Colossians*, 551-552.
  15 Elton, *Colossians*, 553.
  16 Elton, *Colossians*, 554-555.
  17 Elton, *Colossians*, 560-563.
  18 Elton, *Colossians*, 564, 567.
  19 Nicholas Byfield, *An Exposition Upon the Epistle to the Colossians* (London, 1617; repr. 1627), 107.
  20 Byfield, *Colossians*, 116.
  21 Byfield, *Colossians*, 126.
  22 William Gouge, *Domestical Duties* (London, 1622), 302-303.

Chapter 13: *Most blessed assurance*
  1 Thomas Horton, *Forty-Six Sermons on Romans 8* (London: A. Maxwell, 1674), 1.
  2 Horton, *Romans 8*, 2.
  3 Horton, *Romans 8*, 3.
  4 Horton, *Romans 8*, 4-6.
  5 Horton, *Romans 8*, 8.
  6 Horton, *Romans 8*, 8-9.
  7 Horton, *Romans 8*, 10.
  8 Horton, *Romans 8*, 16.
  9 Horton, *Romans 8*, 17.
  10 Horton, *Romans 8*, 26.
  11 Horton, *Romans 8*, 28-29.
  12 Horton, *Romans 8*, 16.
  13 Horton, *Romans 8*, 33,37.
  14 Horton, *Romans 8*, 49.
  15 Horton, *Romans 8*, 56.
  16 Horton, *Romans 8*, 68.
  17 Horton, *Romans 8*, 90.
  18 Horton, *Romans 8*, 91.
  19 Horton, *Romans 8*, 105,108.
  20 Horton, *Romans 8*, 109-110.
  21 Horton, *Romans 8*, 115,122.
  22 Horton, *Romans 8*, 181.
  23 Horton, *Romans 8*, 203.
  24 Horton, *Romans 8*, 204-205.
  25 Horton, *Romans 8*, 216.
  26 Horton, *Romans 8*, 229.
  27 Horton, *Romans 8*, 242.
  28 Horton, *Romans 8*, 255-256.
  29 Horton, *Romans 8*, 279.

30 Horton, *Romans 8*, 295.
31 Horton, *Romans 8*, 361.
32 Horton, *Romans 8*, 362.
33 Horton, *Romans 8*, 375-377.
34 Horton, *Romans 8*, 385.
35 Horton, *Romans 8*, 401.
36 Horton, *Romans 8*, 411.
37 Horton, *Romans 8*, 446.
38 Horton, *Romans 8*, 473.
39 Horton, *Romans 8*, 497.
40 Horton, *Romans 8*, 509.
41 Horton, *Romans 8*, 534.
42 Horton, *Romans 8*, 535.
43 Horton, *Romans 8*, 546.
44 Horton, *Romans 8*, 558.
45 Horton, *Romans 8*, 571.
46 Horton, *Romans 8*, 600-601.

Chapter 14: *Advent to judgement*

1 David Dickson, *An Exposition of all St. Paul's Epistles Together with those other Epistles of the Apostles St. James, Peter, John and Jude* (London, 1659), 32.
2 Dickson, *An Exposition of the Epistles*, 132.
3 Dickson, *An Exposition of the Epistles*, 142.
4 Dickson, *An Exposition of the Epistles*, 150-151.
5 Dickson, *An Exposition of the Epistles*, 151.
6 Dickson, *An Exposition of the Epistles*, 79.
7 Dickson, *An Exposition of the Epistles*, 180-181.
8 Dickson, *An Exposition of the Epistles*, 181.
9 Dickson, *An Exposition of the Epistles*, 176.
10 Dickson, *An Exposition of the Epistles*, 252.
11 Dickson, *An Exposition of the Epistles*, 297.
12 Dickson, *An Exposition of the Epistles*, 311.
13 Dickson, *An Exposition of the Epistles*, 35.
14 Dickson, *An Exposition of the Epistles*, 302-303.
15 Joseph Caryl, *Exposition of the Book of Job* (London, 1676; abridged, Edinburgh: John Berrie, 1836), 123.
16 Caryl, *Job*, 124-125.
17 Iain Murray, *The Puritan Hope* (Edinburgh: The Banner of Truth Trust, 1971), 123.
18 *Westminster Confession of Faith* in Philip Schaff, *The Creeds of Christendom*, 3 vols. (New York: Harper & Brothers, 1877), 3:672-673.

Other titles available from Joshua Press

A foundation for life
A study of key Christian doctrines and their application

Edited by Michael A.G. Haykin

ARE YOU TRYING to understand what the Christian faith is all about? Does studying Christian doctrine seem impractical to your daily life? Do you find some biblical teachings confusing? When things happen in your life do you find yourself questioning God's character? Are you confused about judgment? sanctification? sin? With these and many other questions in our minds, we have brought together some contemporary pastors and church leaders to help explain the basic doctrines of the Christian faith in an easy, understandable way. The impact of these truths should transform your life and help to renew our society.

JOSHUA PRESS / ISBN 1-894400-17-8

Friendship
By Hugh Black

THE HIGH IDEAL to which friendship was held by the ancient writers seems to be an obsolete sentiment today. Western society, with its busyness and self-centredness, to many people, feels like a cold and lonely place. In this culture of cynicism and malaise Hugh Black directs our attention to the importance of friendship and the blessing that it can be. He addresses the challenges and responsibilities associated with friendship including the tragic consequences of wrecked friendships. He defines the limitations of friendship but also highlights the blessings it can bring. In true friendship, accountability and love inspire us to live with more honour, integrity and grace. Ultimately, we see that in Jesus Christ we can have that "higher friendship," which revolutionizes the way we live, the way we think and the things we value.

JOSHUA PRESS
ISBN 978-1-894400-28-2 (HDBK) / ISBN 978-1-894400-27-5 (PBK)

U-turn in the fast lane
One man's journey back to God

Foreword by Paul Henderson
By Rebecca Dye Heron

DON HERON KNEW about God as a child, but now he is trying to drive all that from his mind—he doesn't need God or the crutch of religion. From industrial espionage to the rush of crime, Don's every move seems to distance himself from God. When the swirl of auto theft, easy money, drinking and strip bars comes to a halt with his arrest, Don begins to face the hole he is in and look for the hope he will need to recover his misspent life— and he comes to know the power of God's forgiveness and the joy of a changed life! Don's life in the fast lane is transformed by a radical u-turn in his thinking.

JOSHUA PRESS / ISBN 1-894400-18-6

Fierce the conflict

By Norman H. Cliff

FIERCE THE CONFLICT relates the hardship and struggle of eight believers whose faith was tested through periods of persecution, imprisonment and forced labour in the difficult days of the "Accusation Meetings" and the traumatic ten years of China's Cultural Revolution.
ISBN 1-894400-12-7

Fresh springs
Essays by Tom Wells

TOM WELLS' unusual ability to articulate complex theological issues into layman's terms has made his writings of immense value to the Christian church. These essays provides fresh insight and wisdom into relevant topics such as unity, worship, sanctification and motives for evangelism.
ISBN 1-894400-14-3

When God walked on campus
A brief history of evangelical awakenings at American colleges and universities

By Michael F. Gleason

HERE ARE SOME accounts of revivals in the past two centuries that will whet your appetite for the transforming work of God's Spirit on campuses today. From the halls of Princeton, Yale, Harvard, Dartmouth, Bethel, Wheaton, Trinity, Ashland, and many others, comes stories of awakening and revival. On both secular and Christian campuses, the moving of God was evident as men and women were converted and stirred to ministry and foreign service. Out of these awakenings came the formation of many of the student and campus fellowships still at work today.

JOSHUA PRESS / ISBN 1-894400-16-X

Book and cover design © 2007 Janice Van Eck

Deo Optimo et Maximo Gloria
To God, best and greatest, be glory

www.joshuapress.com

www.ingramcontent.com/pod-product-compliance
Lightning Source LLC
Chambersburg PA
CBHW032000080426
42735CB00007B/462